Spider Monkeys are NOT pets!

Do NOT buy a spider monkey!

Spider Monkeys are NOT suitable as pets but if you DO decide to buy one, regardless of all the problems surrounding these monkeys, please look after it properly, as described in this book.

by

George Hoppendale

Published by IMB Publishing.

All rights reserved.

Table of Contents

Contents

Foreword 8

Chapter I - An Introduction to Spider Monkeys........................11

   1. Old World vs. New World Monkeys....................................12

   2. Natural Habitat of Spider Monkeys.....................................13

      Interaction with Other Animals 13

   3. Physical Characteristics..14

      Life Span 15

      Intelligence 15

      Vocalizations and Threat Displays...................................16

      Color Vision 17

      Locomotion and Movement 17

      Diurnal Foragers..18

   4. Types of Spider Monkeys...19

      Red-faced spider monkey, Ateles paniscus 19

      White-fronted spider monkey, Ateles belzebuth 19

      Peruvian spider monkey, Ateles chamek..........................19

      Brown spider monkey, Ateles hybridus 20

      White-cheeked spider monkey, Ateles marginatus 20

      Black-headed spider monkey, Ateles fusciceps 20

Chapter 2 - Understanding Spider Monkey Society..................22

   1. Social Structure in the Wild 22

      Group Dynamics..22

      Fission-Fusion Groups and Foraging 23

      Social Life 24

   2. Social Structures in Captivity are Dependent on Environment....24

Table of Contents

   3. Social Isolation in Captivity Leads to Marked Abnormal Behavior 26

Chapter 3 - Spider Monkey Conservation 28

   1. Status of Spider Monkeys in the Wild..28

   2. Spider Monkeys in Zoos...29

   3. Rescue Groups..30

Chapter 4 - Adopting a Spider Monkey 32

   1. What to Know Before You Buy a Spider Monkey.....................33

      There Are No Domesticated Monkeys 33

      Transference of Dependence 34

      Aggression with Aging..35

      Monkeys Cannot Be Housebroken 36

      Diapers and Sanitary Supplies...37

      Diaper Changes 37

      Sanitation Issues Are Crucial 38

      Just How Smart is Your Pet Monkey 38

      Monkeys are Destructive...39

      Legal Restrictions May Apply..40

      Insurance Is Imperative 41

   2. Where to Buy a Spider Monkey 42

      Work With a Licensed Breeder or Dealer 42

      Avoid Online and Newspaper Classifieds....................................43

      Warning Signs of Problem Behavior..44

      Veterinary Evaluation Before Adoption.......................................44

      Ethical Considerations to "Rescuing" a Monkey 45

      Average Cost of a Spider Monkey 45

Chapter 5 - Daily Care of Spider Monkeys 46

Table of Contents

1. Habitat Overview 46
   - Minimum Housing Requirement 46
   - Security First 46
   - Don't Neglect Vertical Space 47
   - Think Change 47
   - Elevate Feeding and Drinking Activities 48
   - Include a Containment Space 48
2. Diet and Nutrition 49
   - Selecting Fruits 49
   - Selecting Vegetables 49
   - Food Preparation 50
   - Additional Food 50
   - Where to Buy Monkey Food 51
   - Water 51
   - Foods to Avoid 52
   - Proper Food Storage 52
   - Obesity in Pets is a Major Concern 52
   - Nutritional Guidance May be Difficult to Obtain 53
3. Enrichment - Toys and Intellectual Stimulation 54
4. Daily Handling 55
   - Feeding Schedule 56
   - Enclosure Cleaning 56
   - Use of Harnesses and Leashes 56
   - Transportation 57
   - Play and Interaction 57
   - Managing Aggression and Biting 58
   - Flea Treatment 59

Table of Contents

- 5. Costs 59
- 6. Example of Estimated Costs 61
  - A Word on Expenses 62
  - A Word on Insurance Costs 62
- Chapter 6 - Creating a Spider Monkey Habitat 63
  - 1. Design Considerations 63
    - Indoor vs. Outdoor 63
    - Cage vs. Natural Habitat 64
    - Use of Vertical Space 64
  - 2. Intellectual Stimulation 65
    - Food Puzzles 65
    - Toys 66
    - Sleeping Boxes 67
    - Food and Fresh Water 67
    - Television and Music 67
  - 2. Need for Variety 67
- Chapter 7 - Spider Monkey Health 69
  - 1. Common Illnesses and Conditions 69
    - Obesity, Diabetes, and Hypertension 69
    - Inflammatory Bowel Disease 71
    - Tooth Removal as a Control Measure 71
    - Mental Illness 72
  - 2. Disease Transmission 73
    - Zoonotic Diseases and Transmission Routes 73
    - Monkey to Man 74
    - Man to Monkey 74
    - Introducing New Monkeys to the Household 74

Table of Contents

    Signs of Illness and Disease in Monkeys 75
    Finding a Vet 75
    Routine Veterinary Testing 75
    Vaccinations 76
    Locating a Primate Vet 77
    The Cost of Medical Care 77
Chapter 8 - Spider Monkey Reproduction 79
    1. Courtship 79
    2. Infant Care 79
    3. Death of an Infant 80
    4. Breeding in Captivity 80
    Private Breeding of Spider Monkeys is Discouraged 81
Chapter 9 - Spider Monkey Resources 83
    1. Reference Websites and Materials 83
    2. Supplies and Equipment 85
    3. Support and Discussion Groups 86
Chapter 10 - Conclusion 87
    1. The Blessing and the Problem of Monkey Longevity 87
    2. Forget the Myth of the Dumb Animal 87
    3. Monkeys Don't Always React Well to Strangers 88
    4. Monkeys Are Expensive Pets 89
    5. Health Care for Your Monkey May Be a Challenge 89
    6. Making the Decision to Adopt 89
    7. Prepare Everything in Advance 90
Glossary 92
Appendix I - Pet Monkey Regulations 97

Table of Contents

U.S. Regulations Regarding Spider Monkeys by State-correct at time of printing. 97

U.K. Regulations Regarding Spider Monkeys 102

Appendix II - Primate Sanctuaries 103

    U.S. 103

    U.K. 103

Works Cited 105

Index 108

Foreword

Some people, however many times they read that spider monkeys are not good pets, decide to buy one. This book is a guide of how to make the monkeys as happy as possible in a domesticated environment, knowing that they will never really be happy as they are born to live in the wild.

There really is no "good way" of keeping any monkeys as pets and the spider monkey is no exception. Spider monkeys are strong, wild animals who can cause serious damage if taken away from their natural environment. They can become very scared, very aggressive towards other animals and human beings and often, they end up in very poor health. Too many monkeys die because their owners don't know how to care for them.

A lot of monkeys are bought from the black market but the people buying them don't even know this. Breeders are extremely cruel by ripping away baby monkeys from their mothers when they are only a few weeks old, making it a very distressing experience for the baby monkey and the mum.

Keeping primates as pets is wrong and cruel for the animal. You cannot take a non-domesticated animal and than expect to have a lovely pet like a cat or a dog.

Spider monkeys are unfortunately fast turning into endangered species. People, sadly, are their greatest enemy. People hunt them down for meat and also drag them into lucrative pet trade.

However, despite all this, people still get spider monkeys as pets. This book is for those people. If you DO decide to get a spider

Foreword

monkey, regardless of all the problems surrounding these animals. please make their home as pleasant as possible and please, please, love them dearly.

There you go, I have said it at the beginning of the book that spider monkeys are not to be kept as pets so I advice you NOT to get one but sadly, I know, that some of you reading this book will have one or are planning to get one.

Now I will tell you briefly what you will find in this book.

Any book that attempts an in-depth look at a subject is a daunting endeavor. The keeping of spider monkeys as pets might seem like a simple matter on the face of things.

The opening chapter of this book, which explores the fascinating lives of these creatures in the tropical rain forests of South and Central America, proves otherwise.

No one should attempt to welcome a spider monkey into their home or life without first understanding their social and psychological complexity, which has a direct bearing on their behavior in captivity.

This book provides a thoughtful commentary on the importance of environment, which is crucial to creating an appropriate habitat for a pet spider monkey.

I also focus on how to locate spider monkeys to purchase as pets, the daily care these creatures require, the intricacies of constructing a home environment for them, and the necessity of regular and thorough veterinary care.

You will also find a resource and reference section, which includes common terms, sources for supplies, and owner

Foreword

discussion and support groups, followed by concluding remarks and a Glossary.

Appendix I is a list of legal provisions in the United States and the United Kingdom relevant to keeping spider monkeys as pets.

Appendix II lists primate sanctuaries. Sadly, many pet monkeys are given up as they age. At sexual maturity, monkeys become more aggressive and are often uncontrollable. Zoos will not adopt primates that have been raised as pets, so sanctuaries play a vital role in protecting these animals that, by the circumstances of their raising, really don't act like monkeys.

Where applicable, the text provides information for both the United States and the United Kingdom.

The end result is not just another pet "how to" book, but an honest attempt to prepare any prospective spider monkey owner for the life-long commitment they are undertaking.

Having a spider monkey as a pet is rather like adopting a child. This easily accessible text is a must read for anyone contemplating adopting a monkey. The advice is straightforward and practical and will benefit both sides of the equation — man and monkey.

Chapter 1 - An Introduction to Spider Monkeys

Chapter I - An Introduction to Spider Monkeys

Spider monkeys are one of more than 300 species of primates that exist around the world. They are agile, intelligent, and highly sought after as pets. Where do these clever and winsome little creatures fall in the primate world?

Spider monkeys are the largest of the New World monkeys, weighing in at around 20 lbs. (9.07 kg) and sporting tails that can be as long as 35 inches (89 cm). It is important to understand, however, that not all primates are monkeys.

Non-human primates include apes, monkeys, and prosimians. These creatures range in size from the pygmy mouse lemur, which will fit in the palm of your hand, to massive gorillas that can weigh more than 400 lbs. What makes a primate an ape rather than a monkey?

The general rule of thumb in distinguishing an ape from a monkey is that apes are large and do not have tails. However, there are some monkeys that reach considerable size, and also do not have tails. What all apes do have in common are short, broad noses, whereas monkeys have snouts.

Additionally, apes can create and use basic tools, and they engage in active problem solving. Their social groups are highly complex. Great Apes include chimpanzees, gorillas, bonobos, and orangutans, all of which live in Africa or Asia. The Lesser Apes, gibbons and siamangs, are indigenous to Asia.

All apes are part of the parvorder of higher primates known as catarrhines. They are also "Old World" species. Spider monkeys, which are indigenous to Mexico, South America, and Central America are platyrrhines, and are "New World" monkeys. There are no apes indigenous to the New World.

Chapter 1 - An Introduction to Spider Monkeys

1. Old World vs. New World Monkeys

In describing monkey species, there is a sharp delineation between Old World and New World monkeys. Old World monkeys are physically larger and have opposable thumbs like humans.

They do not have prehensile tails (capable of gripping), so they can sit down. Their nostrils face downward, and they may be terrestrial (living on the ground all or part of the time.)

Old World monkeys include baboons, macaques, and colobus monkeys. They originate in Africa and Asia.

New World monkeys use "hinged" thumbs. They do have tails, and therefore cannot sit down. They are physically smaller, and arboreal, meaning they live in trees. Their nostrils face sideways.

They are typically not aggressive to humans in the wild, although this is not true of captive monkeys. Unlike their Old World counterparts, however, New World monkeys do not respond aggressively to direct eye contact.

New World monkeys include:

- marmosets and tamarins (family *Callitrichidae*)
- capuchins and squirrel monkeys (family *Cebidae*)
- night or owl monkeys (family *Aotidae*)
- titis, sakis, and uakaris (family *Pitheciidae*)
- howler, spider, and woolly monkeys (family *Atelidae*)

Prosimians or "pre-monkeys" come from Asia and Africa, and include lemurs, lorises, bushbabies, and tarsiers. They are considered to be more primitive than primates and are largely nocturnal. They show fewer cognitive abilities and do not live in complex social arrangements.

Chapter 1 - An Introduction to Spider Monkeys

2. Natural Habitat of Spider Monkeys

There are seven species of spider monkeys. In scientific terms, they belong to the order of primates and the family *Atelidae*, sub-family *Atelines*, genus *Ateles*. They are found from southern Mexico to southeastern Brazil.

Spider monkeys prefer old growth tropical, evergreen, and semi-evergreen environments where they can live in the top layers of the canopy. They will rarely move into areas that have been disturbed by human habitation.

Spider monkeys are frugivorous, consuming 80% to 90% of their daily food intake from fruits. They supplement their diet with seeds, flowers, leaves, bulbs, aerial roots, bark, decaying wood, and honey as well as insects, insect larvae, and bird's eggs.

Their consumption of fruit and seeds plays a vital role in the ecosystem of the tropical rain forest. Spider monkeys actively disperse seeds both through the action of their feeding behavior, and in their feces.

As is so often the case when an ecosystem is interrupted, the spider monkeys and the rain forest they inhabit are caught in a deadly cycle of destruction. Deforestation, logging, hunting, and the pet trade are damaging the spider monkey's native environment and thinning the number of animals present.

As the spider monkey population declines, the forest is even less capable of recovering from manmade incursions because the monkeys are not re-seeding the plants on which they would normally feed.

Interaction with Other Animals

As a further example of the harmony with which spider monkeys interact with their natural environment, there have been reports of

Chapter 1 - An Introduction to Spider Monkeys

individual spider monkeys cultivating relationships with other primates, particularly capuchin monkeys. However, when other bands of monkeys come into contact with a spider monkey band, the two generally ignore one another and show no aggression.

When spider monkeys encounter other animals, the monkeys may exhibit the kind of branch shaking/breaking and barking vocal displays common to the species' threat display. Mainly this happens when terrestrial animals gather below where spider monkeys are feeding to eat the fruit dropped by the monkeys.

Opportunistic feeders (who may even follow foraging bands of spider monkeys) may include other rain forest dwellers like agoutis, deer, peccaries, various birds, and even the jungle tortoise.

3. Physical Characteristics

Although each species of spider monkey has some unique characteristics, in general, these monkeys weigh from 15-20 lbs. (7-9 kg) irrespective of gender. From the top of their head to the point where their tails begin, spider monkeys are 15-24 inches (38-61 cm) tall. Their hairless tails measure from 20 to 35 inches (51-89 cm) in length, and include a ridged area on the underside of the tip that resembles a fingerprint. This friction pad aids in gripping.

Spider monkeys use their tails to enhance their swinging motion through the trees, and they also engage in suspensory feeding, hanging by nothing but their tails as they gather fruit. In most descriptions, the spider monkey's tail is referred to as the animal's "fifth hand." Spider monkeys are extremely agile. Only the gibbon exceeds them in physical prowess.

Their hairless faces are either pink or black, with distinct rings around the eyes. The hair covering the body is coarse and shaggy, running from reddish brown to black by species. Both the hands

Chapter 1 - An Introduction to Spider Monkeys

and feet are normally black, and the limbs are exaggerated and spindly (thus the name "spider.")

Spider monkeys are one of the few primate species that lack thumbs, or, if a thumb is present, it will be functionless. They do, however, have five toes.

Life Span

Predation rates among spider monkeys in the wild are high, which explains why they prefer to live in the upper canopy of the rain forest as much as 90-98 feet (30 meters) above the jungle floor.

At lower levels, they easily fall prey to a variety of animals, including man. Infants, who remain completely dependent on their mothers for up to 10 months, are especially vulnerable.

Some spider monkey species are regarded as endangered. The monkeys have suffered heavily from deforestation, hunting, the pet trade, and outbreaks of malaria.

Spider monkeys can live for 25-30 years. They reach sexual maturity at age 6-7, at which time females generally give birth for the first time. Females typically produce one offspring every 37 months, since they take 3 years to completely wean their babies.

Intelligence

Spider monkeys are regarded as the most intelligent of all the New World monkeys. In a 2007 study, it was determined that they are the third most intelligent primate behind orangutans and chimpanzees. They beat gorillas and all other monkeys.

Chapter 1 - An Introduction to Spider Monkeys

Spider monkeys learn and adapt quickly, showing signs of possessing excellent and functional memory. This may be an evolutionary adaptation to their fruit-based foraging diet, which requires them to memorize and to recognize a wide range of edible items both by type and location.

People who attempt to train spider monkeys say the monkey can be tricked once into performing a specific behavior, but won't fall for the same inducement again. This is, however, one of the most delightful aspects of keeping a spider monkey as a pet. They can be taught to do virtually anything, and are inquisitive problem solvers by nature.

Vocalizations and Threat Displays

Spider monkeys produce a range of vocalizations. These include short, abrupt "barking," a sound similar to a horse's whinny, and prolonged screams. When threatened, a spider monkey will move to the end of the branch on which it is standing, shake the leaves, and bark in an attempt to drive away the intruder. They have been known to drop branches on the heads of other animals and even humans. Additionally, the monkeys will both defecate and urinate to repel attackers.

Scientists have also studied long-range calls used by spider monkeys that seem to convey messages about territory and location. Only male spider monkeys emit these "long calls" that can be heard for 800-1000 meters on the forest floor, and as much as 2000 meters within the canopy. Spider monkeys are able to vary their vocalizations to the point where individual recognition is possible among foraging groups.

A band of spider monkeys (typically 30-70 individuals) will break up during the day into feeding parties. Long-range calls between individuals who can recognize one another may be used to coordinate changes in the size and composition of the foraging

Chapter 1 - An Introduction to Spider Monkeys

groups throughout the day. Mothers and their offspring seem to have a similar degree of vocal complexity in their interactions.

Color Vision

Most female spider monkeys are trichromatic. They can see blue, green, and red. About 40% are dichromatic and can see only blue and green. No male spider monkey can see the color red.

Some studies have shown that male spider monkeys will reject red elements in their environment, which should be taken as a cue by handlers and owners that a color that grabs the attention of humans may mean nothing to these animals.

Locomotion and Movement

Spider monkeys move through the trees using a hand-over-hand motion known as brachiation. They also use their long, prehensile tails to steady their progress, preventing side-to-side swaying by grasping branches for stabilization. This allows them to move more efficiently and with less wasted effort.

Their passage through the high canopy of the trees is marked by acrobatic and rapid leaps. A single arm stride may propel a spider monkey as much as 40 feet (12.19 meters). They can also move in a quadrupedal fashion, utilizing all four limbs. Other forms of movement or climbing include bridging (often used by adult females who form a living bridge across which younger, less capable monkeys can pass), pull-ups, lowering, and swinging.

Within the canopy, spider monkeys may hold on to a branch and walk upright on two legs over a short distance. On the rare occasions when they descend to the ground, they can walk on two legs, holding their tails stiff against their backs.

Chapter 1 - An Introduction to Spider Monkeys

Some movements are reserved for play only. For instance, young spider monkeys will hang upside down and use all four limbs to move along branches, a behavior in which adults rarely engage.

When resting in the canopy, spider monkeys will sit on a branch so their tails can hang out of the way (or grasp a nearby support), stand (and potentially lean), and hang suspended using their tails to hold themselves in place. If they're going to rest for a long period, they recline.

Diurnal Foragers

Spider monkeys are awake and active during the day, spending about 80% of their time foraging, or traveling between spots where food is available. At night, they sleep high in the trees, favoring forked branches as their "bedrooms."

This helps to explain one of the key challenges of keeping monkeys in captivity. They simply get bored. Spider monkeys get up every morning and go to "work." Their society is so sufficiently complex that they cooperatively manage the use of food resources in their area.

Spider monkeys don't want to be fed from dishes, or given a life of ease. They want to search for their food, and they want to be working with one another. Their life as foragers has honed their mental skills of recognition and retention. Take away the foraging behavior, and you miss out on witnessing how intelligent they really are. The search for food can be a great opportunity for you to create an environment in their enclosure that encourages that behavior. Your pet monkey can be endlessly entertained and inquisitive with very little effort. Look for ways to increase its ability to problem solve.

Chapter 1 - An Introduction to Spider Monkeys

4. Types of Spider Monkeys

There are seven species of spider monkeys, most of which are considered vulnerable, endangered, or critically endangered in the wild.

Red-faced spider monkey, Ateles paniscus

Although named the red-faced spider monkey, the face of this species is pink. These monkeys are also known as the Guiana spider monkey or red-faced black spider monkey. They are indigenous to the rain forests of northern South America. Their conservation status on the IUCN Red List of Threatened Species is "vulnerable." Averaging around 20 lbs. (9.1 kg) in weight and a length of 21.7 inches (55.2 cm), these pink-faced monkeys are covered in long, black hair. They were classified in 1858 by Swedish botanist and zoologist Carl Lennaeus.

White-fronted spider monkey, Ateles belzebuth

The white-fronted spider monkey, also known as the white-bellied or longhaired spider monkey is indigenous to the northwestern Amazon in Columbia, Ecuador, Venezuela, Peru, and Brazil. Averaging about 20 lbs. (9.1 kg) in weight, these endangered monkeys have a pale belly, and a forehead patch with an orange to buff coloration. They were first classified in 1806 by French naturalist Étienne Geoffroy Saint-Hilaire.

Peruvian spider monkey, Ateles chamek

The Peruvian spider monkey is indigenous to Peru, Brazil, and Bolivia. They are typical in size to other spider monkeys, but their tails can be as long as three feet (1 meter). They are very similar in appearance to red-faced spider monkeys, having pinkish faces and long black hair. Like others of their kind, the

Chapter 1 - An Introduction to Spider Monkeys

Peruvian spider monkey is endangered. Prussian naturalist and explorer Alexander von Humboldt classified these monkeys in 1812.

Brown spider monkey, Ateles hybridus

The critically endangered brown spider monkey is found in Northern Columbia and Northwestern Venezuela. In the past, they have been treated as a sub-species of the white-fronted spider monkey (*Ateles belzebuth*) or of Geoffroy's spider monkey. Blue eyes occasionally appear in this species. These monkeys were first classified in 1829 by Étienne Geoffroy Saint-Hilaire.

White-cheeked spider monkey, Ateles marginatus

The white-cheeked spider monkey, which is indigenous to Brazil, has been on the endangered list since 2008. They suffer most in the wild from hunting and loss of habitat. They are similar in size to all other species of spider monkey, but have distinctive white patches on their faces. They were classified by Étienne Geoffroy Saint-Hilaire in 1809.

Black-headed spider monkey, Ateles fusciceps

The black-headed spider monkey is found in Central and South America, Columbia, Nicaragua, and Panama. Its sub-species include the brown-headed spider monkey (*Ateles fusciceps fusciceps*) and the Colombian spider monkey (*Ateles fusciceps rufiventris*). The black-headed spider monkey is critically endangered having sustained a population loss in excess of 80% over the past 45 years. This species was classified in 1866 by British zoologist John Edward Gray.

Chapter 1 - An Introduction to Spider Monkeys

Geoffroy's spider monkey, which is indigenous to Central America, parts of Mexico, and a small portion of Columbia is one of the most active and agile of the species. It climbs and leaps more than any other spider monkey. Its subspecies include the Yucatan spider monkey (*Ateles geoffroyi yucatanensis*), the Mexican spider monkey (*Ateles geoffroyi vellerosus*), the Nicaraguan spider monkey (*Ateles geoffroyi geoffroyi*), and the Ornate spider monkey (*Ateles geoffroyi ornatus.*) With a black face, hands, and feet, Geoffrey's spider monkey is covered in long reddish brown hair. It is endangered, and was first classified in 1820 by the German naturalist and zoologist Henirich Kuhl.

Chapter 2 - Understanding Spider Monkey Society

Spider monkeys are highly social creatures that live in sophisticated societal structures based on fission-fusion dynamics. How these animals behave in the wild, however, is not how they behave in captivity. Their social interactions and individual actions are based largely on the quality of their environment.

1. Social Structure in the Wild

Spider monkeys live in "bands" that are divided daily into sub-groups for the purpose of foraging. In captivity, spider monkeys should never be housed alone. Sadly, however, as pets, these gregarious creatures are often consigned to a solitary existence.

Spider monkeys do not derive the same level of social interaction from humans that they would from others of their own kind, although pet spider monkeys may become neurotically bonded to their keepers. Invariably, isolation in captivity results in some degree of abnormal behavior ranging from anxiety and depression to outright aggression.

Group Dynamics

Spider monkey groups in the wild range in size from 30 to 70 individuals. Males stay in their birth or "natal" group, but when females reach sexual maturity at age 6 or 7, they disperse.

Typical spider monkey communities are made up of related males and unrelated females. Most social interaction takes place between males, but females often lead foraging parties. It is not unusual for a female to be the band alpha or dominant monkey.

Chapter 2 - Understanding Spider Monkey Society

Fission-Fusion Groups and Foraging

Spider monkey bands rarely spend the majority of their time together. Individual animals use about 80% of their waking hours foraging. To maximize the nutritional potential of their territory, foraging parties break off daily from the main group, to go in search of food.

These subgroups vary widely in composition. Usually they are mixed gender, but all-male groups do occur. The size of a foraging party depends entirely on the available food supply, and may be just three or four individuals. Subgroups merge and split regularly.

Evidence continues to grow that spider monkey foraging is a more organized activity than originally suspected. Groups appear to communicate with one another at a distance with long-range calls that may coordinate movement and feeding location.

Although spider monkeys are fruit eaters, a study conducted in Bolivia in 2004 found that their diet is not geared toward maximizing energy. These highly visual foragers retain an impressive amount of information about their food supply, and aim for a daily target of protein consumption.

This natural evaluation of consumed foods supports the idea that although the fission-fusion model of the monkeys' daily lives would seem to suggest individualized feeding by groups, the whole band is likely to be working together to rotate who eats what, when, and where.

The very complexity of the foraging life of spider monkeys accounts for their high level of intelligence, and their ability to watch, learn from what they see, and apply problem-solving skills.

Chapter 2 - Understanding Spider Monkey Society

Social Life

Unlike other monkey species, spider monkeys do not routinely groom one another. Two monkeys who are familiar will embrace on meeting. Studies have found that in spider monkey bands, embraces occur three times more often than grooming.

The typical pattern of a greeting between two familiar spider monkeys will be a mutual chest sniff, usually initiated by the younger monkey.

Male spider monkeys embrace heartily, but females tend to "air kiss" instead of engaging in a full-blown hug. Individuals may also exchange "face greetings" at a distance accompanied with a vocalization that sounds like a whinny.

Monkeys who do not know one another do not embrace, and they do not share food. Monkey "pals" will "co-feed," which basically means they "do lunch."

In captivity, monkeys living communally in zoo exhibits naturally band together for companionship and security. It is heartwarming to watch.

2. Social Structures in Captivity are Dependent on Environment

In a zoo setting, the most successful captive bands of spider monkeys live in conditions with features that attempt to replicate their native environment. Naturalistic exhibits have replaced the old concrete cages where bored animals lived with no stimulation, forced to be on display to the public at all times.

When zoos introduced outdoor exhibits, a process of trial and error began. Initially, monkeys reacted to the increased space with interest and enthusiasm, but within days tended to find

Chapter 2 - Understanding Spider Monkey Society

secluded spaces to hide, creating the problem of "off display" time.

No matter how much good work zoos perform in terms of animal conservation, they still exist on the profits from visitors who come to see animals, not to stare at empty enclosures. (It is to the credit of many zoos, however, that some animals are only placed in their enclosures for limited periods during the day or week because the stress of being on display at all times is too difficult for them.)

Researchers began to experiment with ways to stimulate the monkeys by using their natural behavioral patterns. In the wild, spider monkeys travel widely to forage for food. When they find edible items, they expend effort to obtain them.

Rather than simply feeding the captive monkeys, their keepers began to design hanging food "puzzles," which led to more suspensory feeding on the part of the monkeys.

(This research has led to the development and sale of commercial feeder products for private monkey owners that include intellectual enhancements. There are many "do it yourself" plans for such devices available online, most of which can be constructed out of cheap and readily available PVC piping. A good source of information on this topic can be found at zookeepersjournal.com.)

When the floor of an exhibit is covered with leaves, straw, wood chips, or hay, and food is hidden under the material, monkeys will spend hours looking for something to eat, even when they've consumed everything that was put out. By scattering food throughout an exhibit in small amounts that are less accessible, the monkeys are more alert and interested.

Now, it is standard procedure to use sculpted floors, trees, intertwined ropes and nets, and unanchored branches to make the environment as challenging as possible. This not only increases the amount of "on display" time, but it also feeds the monkeys' intellect and prevents boredom and depression.

This is, however, a never-ending challenge. Spider monkeys are both physically and mentally quick. They learn easily, and they don't forget. A captive monkey's environment must be changed constantly, and new challenges introduced, if the animal is going to act and live like a monkey, and not simply a well-fed captive.

3. Social Isolation in Captivity Leads to Marked Abnormal Behavior

The fact that spider monkeys are so intelligent makes them especially susceptible to psychological stress in captivity. Their anxiety can be generated from a number of sources, both societal and environmental. An important part of keeping captive spider monkeys is managing their stress levels, especially if the animal is living in isolation rather than with a group.

Researchers have found that, like humans, spider monkeys do not do well when they feel they have no control over their lives. Stress reactions range from hyperactive, agitated behavior to lethargic boredom and hiding. Monkeys may become aggressive in the presence of unknown noises and visitors, and, as they would in the wild, use their feces and urine as weapons.

Stress levels are affected by the size and complexity of their enclosure, but studies suggest that although spacious habitats are best, monkeys live more happily in well-designed environments that seek to replicate their native circumstances.

Unfortunately, for private owners, there is often no answer for the problem of social isolation in captive animals. In the wild, spider monkeys derive companionship from their bands, and even in zoos, individuals exhibit high stress reactions when separated from their friends. Spider monkey bands engage in alloparenting,

Chapter 2 - Understanding Spider Monkey Society

where group members assist parents in rearing infants. As much as humans care for their pets, there are certain bonds they cannot replicate simply because they are humans and not monkeys.

There is also the problem that some spider monkeys develop severe separation anxiety, making it difficult for their keepers to leave them alone because they become destructive and noisy. Often the solution on the part of the equally stressed owner is to confine the monkey to an even smaller space, which only increases the animal's anxiety.

It is not unusual for pet spider monkeys to be given up when they reach sexual maturity at age 6 or 7. Then, they are no longer cute babies, but aggressive adults with surging hormones. At that point, however, they also have a full catalog of abnormal behaviors and habits cultivated during their years as pets. No zoo will take them because they literally do not behave as monkeys. Many are rescued by refuges and sanctuaries, but just as many tragically wind up being sold for research.

(To learn more about monkey sanctuaries, see Appendix II.)

Chapter 3 - Spider Monkey Conservation

Seven varieties of spider monkeys living from southern Mexico to Brazil are listed by the International Union for the Conservation of Nature (IUCN) as facing some degree of threat. In addition to environmental hazards like deforestation, spider monkeys are the subjects of a thriving pet trade.

Once in the hands of humans, these creatures face different dangers. Adopted as cute infants weighing only a few pounds, they grow into strong and often aggressive adults of 24 lbs. (10.6 kg) on average. At that point, many owners are forced to give up the monkeys when they can no longer control them. Since zoos will not accept former pets, these monkeys pass into the hands of rescue groups that seek to allow them to live as "normally" as possible for the rest of their lives.

For many captive monkeys, the best place they can be is a well-maintained zoo where a habitat has been constructed with their particular needs and preferences in mind. Although zoo animals are often stressed by being "on display," such facilities also play a vital role in protecting species that are so endangered in the wild they may no longer be able to survive without the intervention of man.

1. Status of Spider Monkeys in the Wild

The major sources of threat to spider monkeys in the rain forest are deforestation and hunting by humans. The monkeys, due to their size, are regarded as a food source by native populations and they are also captured by dealers at a young age for the highly profitable pet trade.

The forests that spider monkeys call home are being whittled away by timber harvesting and land clearance for agricultural

Chapter 3 - Spider Monkey Conservation

purposes. Deforestation reached its critical peak in 2004. Since that time, conservation efforts have led to a 23% decrease in clearance rates, but a great deal of damage has already been done.

Rain forests that once covered 14% of the earth's surface now account for just 6%, yet those critical acres shelter more than half of the total animal species on the earth. Left unchecked, deforestation could completely destroy the rain forests and the animals that live there over an estimated period of 40 years.

The most effected spider monkeys listed on the IUCN Red List of Threatened Species are:

- White-bellied Spider Monkey (*Ateles belzebuth*) - Endangered
- Black-faced Spider Monkey (*Ateles chamek*) - Endangered
- Brown-headed Spider Monkey (*Ateles fuscicieps*) - Critically Endangered
- Geoffroy's Spider Monkey (*Ateles geoffroyi*) - Endangered
- Variegated Spider Monkey (*Ateles hybridus*) - Critically Endangered
- White-cheeked Spider Monkey (*Ateles marginatus*) - Endangered
- Guiana Spider Monkey (*Ateles paniscus*) - Vulnerable

2. Spider Monkeys in Zoos

People who are interested in spider monkeys can learn a great deal from the work being done in zoos both to house captive animals and to improve their circumstances in the wild. If you decide that owning a monkey is more daunting than you may have imagined, supporting the work of professionals is an excellent way to be involved in bettering the lives of these delightfully intelligent and captivating creatures.

Also, studying spider monkey and primate habitats at zoos can help owners to develop betters plans for building a spider monkey enclosure and for varying the intellectual stimulation the pet monkey receives on a daily basis.

The San Diego Zoo Global program, for instance, maintains an active partnership with Nature and Culture International for the preservation of the tropical forests of Mexico and South America. This work includes the biological study of animals and plants in Ecuador and Peru, and is geared toward saving large tracts of land that might otherwise be lost.

The zoo has been involved with monkeys since it's founding in 1916. By 1925, some 22 primate species were represented there. Long a haven for endangered animals, the zoo not only creates premier environments for their resident monkeys, but also works in conservation efforts in the wild.

The Association of Zoos and Aquariums in the United States helps its members to design Species Survival Plans (SSP). Participating zoos treat their collections as a single unit, matching breeding pairs from location to location for the maximum benefit of the species and to preserve genetic vigor.

Numerous zoos in the U.S. have SSPs for spider monkeys, including, but not limited to: San Diego, St. Louis, Central Florida, Palm Beach, Abilene, Los Angeles, Birmingham, and Milwaukee.

3. Rescue Groups

There are numerous rescue groups at work in the United States and Great Britain that seek to alleviate the suffering of primates. These animals may be former pets that could no longer be kept at the homes into which they were adopted, or they may be liberated research animals.

Almost all of these organizations are involved in some way in seeking better laws regulating the acquisition and breeding of

Chapter 3 - Spider Monkey Conservation

primates, and most maintain some kind of educational presence in their communities.

Whenever possible, rescue centers for exotic animals are located in rural areas. Regardless of the species they are fostering, sanctuaries erect buildings and use the acreage available to them in species-specific ways. For monkeys, this means spacious indoor and outdoor living areas appropriate for the climate that allow the animals the control they crave over their day-to-day existence.

Rescue groups and sanctuaries operate on the donations of benefactors and are constantly in need of funds, supplies, and volunteers.

(See Appendix II for a list of sanctuaries and rescue groups.)

Chapter 4 - Adopting a Spider Monkey

The decision to adopt a spider monkey should not be taken lightly. The level of responsibility being assumed is not unlike adopting a child. Spider monkeys are not and cannot be domesticated. They require daily care, and constant supervision. They are prone to abnormal and often aggressive behavior in captivity.

Most of the adorable monkeys you see on TV and in the movies are infants. They are more compliant, receptive to wearing diapers, and are not yet influenced by hormones. In the wild, spider monkey babies stay near their mothers for up to four years, even if she has given birth again.

In captivity, spider monkeys transfer that degree of dependence to their human "parents." If spider monkeys stayed at that stage of their development, they would be much easier pets, but, like human children, they grow up and become "teenagers."

With humans, however, adolescence is eventually over. After age 6 or 7, when spider monkeys have reached sexual maturity, they are essentially perpetual teenagers. They can and do over-react, and often lash out for no reason. Fully adult monkeys are much harder to control than infants.

Just as not every person is cut out to be a parent, not every person is cut out to own a pet monkey. Do NOT buy a spider monkey on a whim. It is imperative for you and for the monkey that you know exactly what you are doing before you proceed.

Chapter 4 - Adopting a Spider Monkey

1. What to Know Before You Buy a Spider Monkey

Unlike dogs, cats, and other domestic animals that have adapted over the centuries to live peacefully and happily with humans as companions and work animals, monkeys remain wild. At some point all domesticated companion species chose to live with humans because there was an advantage to them doing so.

Dogs are pack animals with an innate desire to please their pack leader or "alpha." This level of loyalty easily transferred to human companions until the dog became man's best friend. Cats chose to live near humans because rats and mice were more plentiful around settlements and towns. Humans welcomed the cats to get rid of the vermin.

Monkeys, on the other hand, have no need to live with humans. Because the species has no real history of domestication, spider monkeys are still monkeys no matter where they are living. Essentially they have not "compromised" any of their habits or preferences in the interest of living in a mutually beneficial relationship with humans.

This doesn't mean spider monkeys can't be good pets, but it does mean that the humans who share their lives with them have to work harder to understand how and why the monkeys think and act as they do.

There Are No Domesticated Monkeys

It's no mystery why humans are attracted to the idea of having a pet spider monkey. The animal's clever abilities to learn and to assimilate information, coupled with their engaging personalities, make them absolutely adorable.

In many cases, spider monkeys function well in the presence of humans, especially those monkeys that are born in captivity and have been raised by humans. This is not to say, however, that monkeys aren't challenging companions. Keeping a pet monkey happy and healthy is an ongoing, difficult assignment that can be financially and emotionally expensive.

While there are no domesticated monkeys, all monkeys are smart. They easily learn routines, and because they are social, they do form relationships with humans. It is important to realize that when a monkey is taken from its mother at a young age, the animal has an emotional need to form a new attachment.

If properly cared for by a human, the monkey will see that person as the "mother," clinging to them, and staying close by for protection and affection. This is not true domestication, however, and as the monkey grows, it will be less dependent.

The more you understand how to treat your monkey like a monkey, the greater chance you have of building a successful relationship with your pet.

Never, however, lose sight of the fact that no matter how docile and loving it is, your monkey will always be a wild animal – even if it has been born and raised in captivity.

Transference of Dependence

Baby monkeys remain completely dependent on their mothers for 6-10 months, but unfortunately, it is in this exact period of life that the animals are at their most adorable and adoptable stage.

Many young spider monkeys transfer the dependence they would naturally feel for their mothers to their human caretakers. They can develop severe separation anxiety and often cannot be left alone.

Since it is rare for there to be more than one monkey kept as a "pet" at a time, these gregarious and social animals are often

Chapter 4 - Adopting a Spider Monkey

lonely. Consequently, they become anxious and unhappy, which leads to even less desirable and uncontrollable behaviors.

In the beginning stages of your relationship with your spider monkey, this dependence is a good thing. It encourages the growth of the bond between you and your new pet. You do not, however, want that dependence to turn into neurotic, anxious behavior.

As the animal grows older, at age 10 to 12 months, it should be comfortable being left alone for a few hours at a time in its enclosure. Always provide your spider monkey with adequate intellectual stimulation. For young spider monkeys, this may include a surrogate "mother."

A large stuffed animal to which the monkey can cling when you are away is an excellent way to curb separation anxiety and to give the monkey what it's really craving – a constant source of comfort and security in its environment.

Aggression with Aging

At sexual maturity, spider monkeys can begin to exhibit aggressive behaviors including biting and scratching. These incidents can rarely be traced to any "trigger," and in most cases leave the baffled owner angry, bloody, and over time, more than a little desperate, especially if the relationship has been loving and compliant up to that time.

Many spider monkey owners are unprepared for this transition to a new level of behavior because they are used to seeing young monkeys on public display and in the media. How owners deal with aggression in older monkeys can make the problem more severe.

When a dog does something "bad" and is scolded, or even "spanked," the animal has an innate sense of guilt. A monkey

Chapter 4 - Adopting a Spider Monkey

will simply get angrier, and will react with more aggression. If your pet is in a bad mood, leave the animal alone until it has calmed down.

Look for patterns in the behavior, and try to find devices or strategies the monkey sees as calming. Do not put the monkey in a smaller enclosure, or immediately go to extremes like having all its teeth removed. It would be far better to surrender the monkey to a rescue group.

Going into the relationship, new spider monkey owners need to understand that at some point, they may have to give up the animal – for its sake, and for their own. There may well come a time when you can no longer keep the monkey. Have a plan for that eventuality – before you adopt.

Monkeys Cannot Be Housebroken

Baby monkeys will allow themselves to be diapered, but as they grow older, they will remove the protective garment and do what they need to do regardless of where they are. They cannot be housebroken, nor can they be persuaded to use a litter box.

Of all the questions you should ask yourself about the pros and cons of owning a spider monkey, one of the most important is simply, "Can I deal with the mess?"

It should be noted that there are always exceptions to these "rules." Some spider monkeys will be compliant about wearing diapers throughout their lives, and will not display aggression. If, however, you are new to the idea of owning a spider monkey, prepare yourself for the worst-case scenario.

It's always better to know how bad a situation could be and be pleasantly surprised when it doesn't happen, than to bury your head in the sand and refuse to look at the reality of the issue.

Chapter 4 - Adopting a Spider Monkey

Diapers and Sanitary Supplies

While the animal is young, owners will need to purchase sanitary supplies in bulk. The most cost effective way to approach this essential item is to shop online. Individual diapers cost about 50 cents USD (roughly 50 pence UK).

In some cases, extra small diapers for premature babies may work for your spider monkey, but the better option will be products made specifically for animals. The best primate diapers are those that are gel filled. The material is designed not to swell as it absorbs water, so the monkey can wear the garment for a longer period of time.

Diaper Changes

In general, the younger an animal is when first diapered, the more easily it will tolerate the garment as it ages. For the first 10 months of a spider monkey's life, the baby will ride on its mother's back. Allowing the monkey to cling to something, for instance a stuffed animal, while it's being changed can help to keep the animal calm.

Use regular infant wipes to clean the monkey, paying careful attention to the area at the base of the tail. If the diaper you are using is made specifically for a monkey, there will be a slit for the tail. If the garment is intended for a premature human baby, you will have to create a small opening for the tail. Keep this opening as small as possible to prevent leakage.

Typically, owners also use colorful diaper covers in addition to the protective garment itself. In a practical sense, the extra layer of clothing helps to keep the monkey from removing the diaper, but aesthetically, the covers are more appealing and look cute on the spider monkey.

When spider monkey babies are very small, they may need to be changed as often as every two hours. Expect to spend as much as $12 (£7.75) a day at this stage of your pet's life. Eventually, you will only need to make 6 to 8 diaper changes a day.

Sanitation Issues Are Crucial

A monkey's enclosure must be cleaned thoroughly on a daily basis, including the use of disinfecting agents. Monkeys are highly excitable, and may defecate or urinate when excited or angry. They also use their own bodily by-products as projectiles.

It is possible that cleaning the enclosure will mean hosing off all aspects of the environment, discarding soiled items, and carrying away bedding and flooring material on a regular basis. Be sure you set aside time every day to perform these chores. Insects and vermin will be attracted to the enclosure if it is not clean, and bacteria and parasitic organisms will thrive.

Monkeys are susceptible to a host of diseases caused by parasites. Some of these diseases can be transmitted to humans. Poorly maintained living quarters facilitate the spread of these organisms, many of which are excreted in the animal's feces. When you clean your monkey's enclosure, you are protecting yourself as well as your pet.

Just How Smart is Your Pet Monkey

Many people who share their lives with a spider monkey say the animals amass a working vocabulary equivalent to that of a four-year-old child.

This ability to use language is so acute that a spider monkey can learn the difference between words like "tail" and "foot," and respond appropriately to complete sentences and questions.

Chapter 4 - Adopting a Spider Monkey

They can be taught reasonably complex commands like "turn on the light" or "hand me the ball." This level of intelligence is certainly not limited to spider monkeys. Capuchin monkeys, for instance, are being trained to work with humans who have spinal cord injuries and other mobility impairments.

The monkeys can be taught to help the disabled with everyday tasks in order to facilitate greater independence. Although this service is still controversial, it does illustrate the primates' capacity for learning.

A spider monkey's intelligence represents the double-edged sword of monkey ownership. These animals can be entertaining and loving pets that behave in an almost human fashion, but they also have a constant need to be entertained. When a monkey gets bored, mayhem can ensue.

Monkeys are Destructive

Some experts suggest that you think of a monkey as a perpetual toddler with incredible agility, strength, and exceptional creativity. The mess a monkey makes is not limited to his elimination needs. If he is looking for amusement, he will surely find it, but it may well be at your expense -- and the monkey gives no thought whatsoever to the consequences of his actions.

All monkey owners have something broken, shredded, dug up, or destroyed all the time. A monkey can never be left unsupervised outside its enclosure. They can and will open anything, from cupboards to the refrigerator. Just as you would protect your child from strangulation by window blind cords, you must do the same for your pet. In addition, keep all electrical cords away from your monkey as well.

This clever ability raises the potential for accidental poisoning, or for the animal to simply eat things it shouldn't. Make certain to remove any poisonous items from within your pet's reach.

Chapter 4 - Adopting a Spider Monkey

Monkeys are as drawn to the lure of junk food as their human counterparts, so much so that obesity and diabetes are major problems for pet primates.

A cat may shred your sofa. A dog may dig up your back yard. A monkey on the loose can trash your house, literally. Are you prepared for the pure mischief that is a pet spider monkey? Will you find the antics a source of delight, or will it drive you half mad?

Legal Restrictions May Apply

In Appendix I of this book, you will find general information and reference sources on legal restrictions that might apply to monkey owners in the United States and the United Kingdom. Regardless of where you live, expect to face a web of potentially conflicting laws, regulations, and rules.

In the United States, the Centers for Disease Control prohibited the importation of monkeys into the country in 1975. Today, the majority of monkeys offered for sale in the U.S. are surplus animals from zoos, laboratories, or private breeders. Monkey ownership is not prohibited in the United Kingdom, but the details and qualifications are left to the discretion of local councils.

By the same token, the federal government in the U.S. does not ban primate ownership, allowing the individual states to resolve the specifics associated with exotic pets. County, city, and even homeowner's association rules may further bar the keeping of a monkey as a pet.

The best policy is to work the legal chain downward. In the U.S., for instance, if your state bans the keeping of monkeys as pets, the issue is immediately resolved.

Chapter 4 - Adopting a Spider Monkey

If your state has a partial ban or does allow the keeping of monkeys, move next to the county in which you live, the city (with special attention to zoning laws), and then to your homeowner's association (HOA) if applicable.

Prospective monkey owners would do well to understand that many people, especially the "authorities" look askance at keeping primates as pets.

Just because you are not specifically forbidden to have a monkey does not mean you will not be prevented from such ownership by a maze of interlocking restrictions. If you really want to have a spider monkey, be prepared to become an advocate for your pet from day one.

Insurance Is Imperative

There are certainly agencies that sell exotic pet insurance. In the United States, for instance, one of the better known is VPI at petinsurance.com. These policies, however, most often cover medical care for the animal, which can be important to defray vet bills. The most critical type of insurance for a monkey owner, however, is a pet liability policy.

When any animal causes injury to another person or damage to their property, the animal's owner is responsible under the accepted doctrine of strict liability. This has led to a burgeoning business in "biting dog" policies, with many underwriters refusing to cover breeds recognized as "dangerous."

Pet liability policies are not just for dogs. Many types of exotic animals including monkeys can be covered in the policy, but there is no set rule about premium prices. Typically an insurance agent will visit the pet owner's home and make an assessment of:

- the type of pet to be insured,
- its' legal status in regard to any required licenses or permits,

Chapter 4 - Adopting a Spider Monkey

- the most recent medical records relative to the animal's care,
- the type of enclosure used and security measures in place,
- and the history of the animal's known behavior.

Insurance coverage will not necessarily be denied if these conditions fail to be satisfactory, but the premium levels assessed will certainly be higher.

As with any type of insurance, if you can gain the coverage in conjunction with other policies, you may qualify for a multiple policy discount. It is also possible that your monkey can be insured with a special rider to your existing homeowners policy.

Explore all the potential avenues to find affordable liability insurance, but do not neglect this important component of monkey ownership. Anyone who is bitten or injured by your pet has an excellent potential lawsuit.

2. Where to Buy a Spider Monkey

Anyone who has ever purchased a purebred domestic animal knows that far too many are born in for-profit squalor where quantity far exceeds considerations of quality. While the news talks more about puppy "mills" than monkey "mills," the ramifications of taking a poorly raised primate into your home can be far more serious.

Spider monkeys are highly intelligent and sensitive animals. Their behavior can be dramatically altered by their life experiences. How and where you purchase your pet spider monkey are equally as important as how you will care for the creature once it has become part of your family.

Work With a Licensed Breeder or Dealer

Since 1975, when the Centers for Disease Control shut down the importation of monkeys into the U.S., all spider monkeys sold are domestically bred and raised. Individuals who wish to adopt a spider monkey as a pet should verify that they are buying from a licensed breeder or dealer.

Any individual or entity that plans to breed, sell, exhibit, or perform research with monkeys must apply for a license with the U.S. Department of Agriculture's Animal and Plant Health Inspection Services. This includes retail pet stores that display monkeys for sale on their premises.

The licensing process involves an initial inspection followed by random checks. Regular veterinary care is a condition of licensing, and regulations apply for such issues as insurance and transportation.

In the United Kingdom, anyone seeking to own a primate of any kind must have a license from their local authority under the Dangerous Wild Animals Act (DWAA) 1976. Breeders must be similarly licensed under the statute, but violations are rife.

Purchasing a monkey from an individual or operation that has undergone a licensing process increases your chances of acquiring a healthy animal that has been well cared for and housed under appropriate conditions. If possible, however, have the monkey evaluated by a veterinarian with a working knowledge of primate care.

Avoid Online and Newspaper Classifieds

It's perfectly possible to go on popular online classified sites or to flip through the newspaper ads and find spider monkeys for sale. Avoid purchasing an animal under these circumstances unless you can verify the legitimacy of the breeder and the conditions under which the animal has been raised and housed.

If you do check out a monkey that is being offered through a classified site, do everything you can to verify the animal's age

Chapter 4 - Adopting a Spider Monkey

and previous behavior issues. Beware of a situation where a harried owner is seeking to unload an older, problem pet.

Taking an older animal on as a pet means you are also taking on its history. Monkeys react strongly to their surroundings, and can come to you with pre-existing psychological problems as a consequence of their environment.

Warning Signs of Problem Behavior

Monkeys that are experiencing stress due to poor housing conditions, a lack of social interaction, disease, or mistreatment will often engage in mindless repetitive tasks. The most common forms of this behavior are pacing and repetitive circular movement – literally walking round and round in a circle.

Pay particular attention to any wounds that might appear on the monkey. Stressed monkeys in captivity will self-mutilate, generally by chewing or gnawing. This is something the animals never do in the wild. If you see a monkey showing signs of bites or scratches, which the owner just writes off to a tiff with another monkey, take that with a pinch of salt. Any monkey that is hurting itself is a monkey that is exhibiting mental stress.

Veterinary Evaluation Before Adoption

Before adopting a spider monkey, ask the person selling the animal to produce documentation about its health and that of any other animals that may be present at the location. If licensing or permits are required in your state, ask to see copies of those as well.

If possible, request that a primate veterinarian evaluate the monkey before you purchase the animal, and insist on being present at the examination. Make sure that the monkey is free of parasites, both internal and external, and that the animal has been tested for diseases like tuberculosis. If a breeder is reluctant to

Chapter 4 - Adopting a Spider Monkey

produce this documentation, or refuses to allow a vet to examine the animal, do not buy the monkey.

Ethical Considerations to "Rescuing" a Monkey

Many well-meaning individuals feel the urge to "rescue" monkeys that are being given up or that have obviously been raised in improper conditions. If you want to help an animal under these circumstances, facilitate its adoption by a sanctuary or a rescue group. Do not bring the monkey into your home.

Pet monkeys are routinely given up for behavioral problems when they reach age 6 or 7. At this stage of their lives, the animals are sexually mature, and their propensity for aggression increases markedly.

The better course of action, should you find monkeys living in sub-standard conditions, is to report the breeder or dealer rather than to try to intervene on behalf of the monkeys on your own. These animals have a complex social and psychological structure and, when maltreated, are in need of specialized care from professionals who understand both their physical and emotional needs.

Average Cost of a Spider Monkey

It's almost impossible to "ballpark" a price range for purchasing a spider monkey since the amounts vary so widely. In the U.S. some animals are sold for as much as $6000 (£3,028) while others go for as little as $2800 (£1,832).

Please see Chapter 5 – Daily Care of Spider Monkeys for a more complete description of what a pet monkey requires in terms of habitat and supplies, and an example breakdown of costs per month.

Chapter 5 - Daily Care of Spider Monkeys

Spider monkeys are labor-intensive pets. In order to stay ahead of illness and disease, especially those associated with parasites, a monkey's enclosure must be cleaned and disinfected daily. Monkeys need both physical and intellectual nourishment to thrive, and owners must be able to accept unpredictable and sometimes aggressive behavior, once the animal has reached sexual maturity.

1. Habitat Overview

Adequate space is essential for a monkey's physical and mental health. In the wild, spider monkeys range over a large territory in their daily search for food. They are arboreal creatures, living high in the rain forest canopy. Building a proper enclosure is not as simple as setting up a big cage and throwing some toys inside.

Minimum Housing Requirement

The absolute minimum height for a spider monkey cage is 6 feet high (1.80m). Spread out horizontally as much as possible. Monkeys need unfiltered sunlight, which is a source of Vitamin D, to stay healthy, but they also will want adequate shade. Include a source of fresh water (preferably running water) in all outdoor enclosures.

Security First

Never underestimate the intelligence of a spider monkey. Although they do lack opposable thumbs, they are still agile and clever creatures. They watch, and they learn. Don't make the mistake of using a simple latch on a monkey's enclosure. He'll

Chapter 5 - Daily Care of Spider Monkeys

escape and be out of control in a heartbeat. Always lock your monkey's cage.

Don't Neglect Vertical Space

Spider monkeys are designed to live 85-90 feet (27 meters) above the ground. They are incredible acrobats who love to swing hand-over-hand, climb, leap, and suspend themselves from branches with their prehensile tails. They spend very little of their time on the ground, so in designing your monkey's enclosure think "up."

Vary the complexity of the vertical space with fixed and mobile features. The more complex and interesting, the better. If possible, include some kind of natural vegetation. Suspend ropes vertically and horizontally and use nets. Place platforms at different levels if practical to do so.

Cover the floor of the enclosure with natural materials like bark, leaves, wood chips, or straw. Make it something you can work with easily, since the material will need to be changed regularly as it becomes soiled.

Think Change

Obviously your monkey's enclosure will be a permanent structure, but the features should be flexible. Monkeys get bored quickly, especially those that are living alone. In the rain forest, spider monkeys are naturally social. Even those that have been bred in captivity are used to high levels of interaction.

Boredom can lead to depression, anxiety, aggression, and even mental illness. It's important to remember that you are working with a pet that has a high level of curiosity, reacts emotionally to what's going on around him, and can display a range of emotions from engaged attention to listless, miserable boredom.

Chapter 5 - Daily Care of Spider Monkeys

Intellectual enrichment and constant variety in the environment aren't just necessary for your monkey's physical wellbeing. You are also responsible for his mental health. When critics of keeping monkeys as pets liken their captivity to solitary confinement, owners should hear that and make sure that is NOT how their pets are being housed.

Elevate Feeding and Drinking Activities

A monkey is not a dog. He doesn't want water and food bowls. Foods should be scattered in the vertical spaces of the enclosure. Monkeys derive intellectual stimulation from looking for what they eat. Remember, the spider monkey is a highly efficient natural forager. Some studies have concluded that it is this very activity that accounts for the animal's exceptional level of intelligence.

By the same token, fresh water should be available, but if possible, provide this from a raised position and have some means of suspension near the water source. Spider monkeys engage in suspensory feeding and drinking — hanging by their tails. They can sit, but usually on limbs where they can drape their tails out of the way, or wrap them around the limb as a means of stabilization.

Include a Containment Space

You will want to have a smaller area to the side, even a conventional wire cage, in which your monkey can be placed while you are cleaning his enclosure. This will prevent the monkey from escaping while you work, or being entirely too "helpful."

Remember, too, that monkeys are territorial. Your pet will see his enclosure as "his" and could react with threat displays of branch shaking, object dropping, or the flinging of feces if he thinks you

Chapter 5 - Daily Care of Spider Monkeys

are invading his space. Better to have the animal contained during housekeeping chores for his benefit and yours.

2. Diet and Nutrition

An adult spider monkey requires about 4.5 lbs. 2 kg.) of food daily. Of that, 80% should be fruit and 20% vegetable. Establish a routine of feeding two times a day. Note that monkeys will always go for "dessert" first, so if you are including any "sweet" treats (which should always be a favorite fruit), give those to the animal last.

Selecting Fruits

A good range of fruits for a healthy spider monkey would include such items as: avocado, bananas, mango, melons (cantaloupe or honeydew), oranges, tomatoes, watermelons, and anything else that is in season.

Spider monkeys like variety. Remember that they are foraging animals. Vary the fruits you give them on a regular basis, and pay attention to the animal's preference. If they don't like mangos, don't waste your time or money.

Don't be afraid to experiment. Remember you are feeding a frugivore. Give your monkey fresh fruits (that have been properly washed) as they come in season and go by what the animal will and won't eat in broadening the selection.

Selecting Vegetables

Spider monkeys will do well on a mixture of carrots, corn on the cob, cucumbers, and lettuce. Since they do not eat as many vegetables as fruits, there is not as much need to vary this portion of their diet.

Chapter 5 - Daily Care of Spider Monkeys

Avoid giving your monkey potatoes, since the skin can be harmful to them, but otherwise, you can take on the same attitude of experimentation. If you introduce a vegetable your monkey likes, then use that vegetable. Again, wash the vegetables, and make sure they are fresh with no sign of mold or decay.

Food Preparation

Store the fruits and vegetables you purchase for your spider monkey in clean, dry containers. Use only fresh produce, and discard everything at the first sign of mold or excessive ripeness.

Don't cut the fruits and vegetables into small pieces. A spider monkey's principle "job" in the wild is to look for food. Scatter the fruits and vegetables throughout the enclosure, preferably in feeders or platforms off the ground. It's not cruel to make your monkey look for his supper. That's actually his idea of a five star meal.

Always include fruits and vegetables that have a firm to hard texture along with softer items. Gnawing on large chunks of food improves the health of the monkey's teeth and gums. It also forces them to eat more slowly, and it gives them something to do for a longer period of time.

Additional Food

About twice a week, give your spider monkey approximately 2 cups (60g) of a commercial monkey "chow" as well as a loaf of bread. While it is not a good idea to feed a monkey nothing but commercial dry food, these preparations have been balanced for vitamin and nutrient delivery and are an important supplement to your pet's fresh diet.

Choose a high-quality dry food designed for a primate, for instance, the Zupreem line of products. A 20 lb. sack of Zupreem

Chapter 5 - Daily Care of Spider Monkeys

Dry Primate Diet costs approximately $45 (£29.06). One sack should last several months. Remember, the bulk of your monkey's diet should be in fresh fruits and vegetables.

Where to Buy Monkey Food

Any place that you buy fruits and vegetables for your family is fine as a source of produce for your monkey. Be aware of all the same concerns about washing fruits and vegetables that apply to humans. Do not treat your monkey as the family garbage disposal. If the fruit is too rotten for you to eat, it's too rotten for your monkey.

For dry foods, you can inquire at local pet or feed stores, but rarely will these locations have monkey chow in stock. Most are willing to order for you, but you may have to buy in bulk. Online sources are increasingly a monkey owner's best bet for affordable dry foods. (See Chapter 9 for more information on supply sources.)

Water

It is imperative that monkeys have fresh water at all times. They often will not use bowls or stagnant ponds of water for drinking. Water containers with tubes outfitted with ball bearings at the end, which the monkey licks to get water, are a standard choice.

Don't be worried about placing water in the "easiest" place for your monkey. These animals engage in both suspensory feeding and drinking. Place the water bowl at a fairly high level in the cage and give the monkey something to hang on to while it drinks, for instance a suspended rope.

The more interesting you make your monkey's environment, the better. Both eating and drinking should be sources not just of physical nourishment, but also of intellectual stimulation.

Chapter 5 - Daily Care of Spider Monkeys

Foods to Avoid

Although bananas are popularly associated with monkeys, they should be used sparingly in combination with a broader variety of fruits. Stay away from high-calories and dense root vegetables like potatoes. (Potato skins are unhealthy for monkeys.) Limit or avoid peanuts altogether.

DO NOT under ANY CIRCUMSTANCES give your pet monkey sweets, chocolates, or alcoholic beverages. Monkeys can become addicted to alcohol just as humans can. Alcohol is not only bad for a spider monkey's health, but it also dramatically increases the animal's tendency to become wild, unpredictable, destructive, and aggressive.

Proper Food Storage

Store all food carefully, and feed your monkey only fresh items. BE WARNED that mold is extremely dangerous to your pet monkey's health. Throw out moldy foods immediately, and make sure no mold is growing in the containers in which the items were kept. Better to throw out the container and start fresh.

Some studies indicate that alfalfa leads to autoimmune disease in monkeys. Avoid using alfalfa as a food or on the floor of the animal's enclosure, and do not feed your monkey commercial rabbit pellet foods that contain alfalfa.

Obesity in Pets is a Major Concern

The problem of obesity in pets of any kind starts with the human, not the animal. Too often people see their pets as substitute children, a transference of emotions that easily occurs with monkeys when they are infants. The indulgence may be lovingly meant, but it can also be deadly. Pet monkeys face the same dietary risks as humans — obesity, heart disease, cancer, diabetes, and degenerative joint diseases among others.

Chapter 5 - Daily Care of Spider Monkeys

According to veterinarians, the major reasons that pet monkeys get fat are:

- diets rich in starches, fats, and sweets,
- a lack of dietary fiber,
- access to an overabundance of food,
- an inactive solitary and sedentary lifestyle,
- an overly constricting enclosure,
- and boredom.

Spider monkeys can easily develop a sweet tooth and, like us, they will greedily consume something they like. Because they are foraging animals, they will eat what is in front of them, reasoning it may not be there tomorrow. They also have an innate urge to "beat the competition", even if there is none.

Monkeys who have been hand-raised may have very poor diets as a result. Like children, they develop their dietary preferences at a young age, and are resistant to change. Also, if the monkey's mother was housed in a small cage or lived in a stressful situation, she may have been subject to hormonal surges that altered her baby's ability to metabolize fat. This is a recognized problem in captive monkeys, and one directly tied to a high instance of diabetes.

Nutritional Guidance May be Difficult to Obtain

All monkey owners agree that finding a veterinarian who will treat their pet is extremely difficult. In terms of diet, the Internet has made the problem of nutritional counseling for captive primates somewhat easier. Owners can reach out to one another via discussion boards and forums (See Chapter 9), and can correspond with monkey experts at zoos and commercial feed manufacturers.

Chapter 5 - Daily Care of Spider Monkeys

Be forewarned that most of these experts will not be in favor of a monkey living alone as a pet. Most will answer questions from owners who are obviously trying to provide the best possible care for the spider monkey, however.

3. Enrichment - Toys and Intellectual Stimulation

Many private owners construct indoor/outdoor enclosures for their monkeys, which is an excellent way to introduce variety into the animal's daily life. Be especially cautious, however, to secure all exterior openings and points of attachment. A bored spider monkey is a premier escape artist.

The easiest and most natural means of enrichment is to feed the monkey in a way that caters to his natural desire to forage. Use grass, hay, and wood chips through which the monkey must comb to find food, and if you have the space, incorporate rocks, and raised platforms.

Other enrichment items might be ropes strung both horizontally and vertically, wood planks for climbing, and tire swings. Include a "nest box," which can be a wooden box or plastic drum, and elevate it off the ground.

There are some companies online that manufacture monkey-specific enrichment items, many of which are "puzzle" feeders. It's common though for owners to construct their own enrichment devices with the "do it yourself" approach. Basically, you are limited only by your imagination, your monkey's preferences and interests, and safety concerns.

Think of your monkey as the smartest toddler you've ever known. If you would not give the item to a child, don't give it to your monkey. The same kinds of concerns about choking that motivate safety regulations with children also apply to spider monkeys.

Chapter 5 - Daily Care of Spider Monkeys

Since monkeys require constant variety, even common household items like a toilet paper roll filled with peanut butter can be a source of amusement.

Other ideas might include:

- Using plastic containers with screw-on lids to hold treats and food. (Choose translucent bottles so the monkey can see the food.)

- Go to a local salvage or Goodwill store and find toddler-safe toys, especially those that make a noise or might include a light.

- Use inexpensive PVC pipe and chains to create easily altered swings and hanging devices.

Spider monkeys can also be highly entertained by a television, but always place the device outside the enclosure and beyond the animal's reach. The monkey can harm and even kill himself if the set were to fall, or if the monkey were to gnaw on the power cords.

4. Daily Handling

Monkeys, like small children, respond well to set schedules. Studies have found that monkeys experience a great deal of stress when they feel they have no control over their environment.

Knowing what to expect, in terms of feeding, cleaning, and interaction can actually be a source of comfort for your pet. Once a routine is established, try not to deviate from the animal's "norm," while still giving him the variety and intellectual stimulation he will crave.

Chapter 5 - Daily Care of Spider Monkeys

Feeding Schedule

Since obesity is often a problem in pet monkeys, it's important to feed your animal a balanced diet, in carefully measured amounts, and on a set schedule. Most owners opt for two feedings daily, one in the morning, and one in the late afternoon or early evening. Restrict treats, and do not allow your monkey to get hooked on junk food, which they will readily do if given the opportunity.

Enclosure Cleaning

Because monkeys are susceptible to parasitic disease, and because some of those illnesses can be passed on to humans, it is imperative to clean your monkey's enclosure daily. This routine should involve the use of disinfectant.

It's best to remove or isolate the monkey during the cleaning routine so the job can be thorough and uninterrupted. Remove all traces of urination and defecation, all uneaten food, and any soiled materials.

Change bedding routinely to discourage vermin like fleas and ticks from becoming an issue for your pet — and for you. Additionally, do not allow stagnant water to build up in the enclosure, which is just an invitation for an infestation of mosquitos.

Use of Harnesses and Leashes

There are several approaches to the use of restraining devices with spider monkeys. Collars are not out of the question, although many owners believe their use is cruel, and raises too great a chance of choking. Certainly, a monkey should never be left unattended while wearing a collar.

Chapter 5 - Daily Care of Spider Monkeys

There are also waist collars, which allow a somewhat safer means of control. Bear in mind, however, that monkeys are expert climbers, and simply getting their limbs off the ground is not enough to keep them from grasping an object and refusing to move. Their tail is as flexible and as strong as an additional limb.

A highly popular means of controlling a monkey is to use a harness that actually resembles a vest. This method puts no undo strain on any part of the monkey's anatomy, but allows for the secure placement of a leash. Note that purchasing these harnesses requires the owner to take a measurement of the neck, chest, and belly.

Expect to spend less than $25 (£16.19) for any of these pieces of equipment.

Transportation

Although it is a romantic notion to think about walking around with your monkey on your shoulder, it's always best to transport the animal in a pet carrier. Monkeys are naturally excitable, and often respond negatively to unexpected or unusual sounds. They are even capable of taking a dislike to someone or something on sight. Because monkeys respond to threats with aggressive displays, it's better for the animal, and for anyone near the animal, if the monkey is safely confined.

Play and Interaction

Remember that your pet is, by nature, a social animal. Spider monkeys need interaction, and often suffer from depression and anxiety when they don't get it. Try to balance the amount of time you spend with your pet with those times when the animal needs to be entertaining himself with toys and the features in its enclosure.

Chapter 5 - Daily Care of Spider Monkeys

Spider monkeys have a tendency to get overly attached to their owners and suffer from bouts of separation anxiety. Most monkey owners report that they cannot leave their monkey with an unfamiliar caretaker, which can place real limitations on family or personal scheduling.

The more people your monkey knows, and with whom it interacts successfully, the better as there will be times when you have to go away from home leaving your monkey in the care of another person.

Play also familiarizes you with your monkey's likes and dislikes. You will know what intrigues the animal and what annoys it. Always provide this kind of information to anyone who may be taking care of your monkey for any period of time. Give specific instructions, "He doesn't like it when you make this sound" or "You can always get his attention when you do this."

Spider monkeys have very distinct and often captivating personalities. Most owners have more difficulty tearing themselves away from playtime than trying to work it in. Playtime with your monkey not only builds your relationship with the animal, but also gives you valuable insights into its behavior and tastes.

Managing Aggression and Biting

As with any animal, when a monkey is visibly upset and displaying aggression, back away and leave the creature alone. Do nothing to antagonize or threaten the monkey. If practical to do so, don't interact with the monkey until it calms down.

Remember that you are dealing with an intelligent creature capable of expressing its anger in a targeted way. Any attempt to forcibly "discipline" an already agitated monkey will likely backfire.

Chapter 5 - Daily Care of Spider Monkeys

Typically, spider monkeys express their displeasure by shaking something nearby, throwing items (including their own feces), urinating, and screeching. However, if sufficiently antagonized, a spider monkey will bite and they are well equipped to inflict serious harm.

Immediately seek medical attention for yourself or for the victim of a monkey bite. The wound must be appropriately cleaned, and antibiotics and other drugs administered. There will be a high risk of infection, and if the bite is sufficiently severe, surgery may be required to close the wounds.

All monkey owners report having been scratched or bitten at some point — often without warning — and biting behavior is one of the main reasons cited for giving up a pet spider monkey.

Flea Treatment

Do not use commercial flea treatments on your pet monkey. These products, many of which have proven to be unsafe for small dogs and cats, are definitely not safe for your spider monkey. Always treat the enclosure for fleas, not the monkey. In general, bathing the monkey regularly, maintaining your yard, and keeping the animal's habitat clean should be sufficient to prevent fleas from being an issue.

5. Costs

As with almost any pet, calculating the complete cost of owning a spider monkey is extremely difficult. Beyond the initial expense of acquiring the monkey, which could range as high as $6000 (£3,028), you should consider the cost of setting up the animal's habitat, and caring for it on a daily basis.

Your best strategy is to draw up a list of all the things involved in becoming a spider monkey owner, and pricing the essentials in your area to achieve an estimated total.

Chapter 5 - Daily Care of Spider Monkeys

Such a list would include (but not be limited to) the following:

- the monkey itself
- an enclosure that works in your available space
- modifications to your home to accommodate the enclosure (for instance giving the monkey indoor/outdoor access)
- enhancement equipment for the habitat like swings, nets, ropes, nesting boxes and other items discussed previously
- toys and other intellectual stimulants including a television or radio
- bedding and floor lining material for the enclosure (hay or wood chips, for instance)
- one month of food including fresh fruits and vegetables, bread, and commercial monkey chow
- restraint devices including a harness and carrier for transportation
- veterinary care including travel to and from the office if it is not local

Always factor in emergency expenses like repairs to the enclosure, or unexpected vet bills.

Discuss your planned acquisition with your insurance professional. Many dog owners are forced to take out extra coverage because they own a breed that is considered dangerous or aggressive. Monkey bites are as serious or more so than dog bites. Are you prepared to cover the medical expenses of anyone who might be harmed in your home?

Finally, consider that finding someone to "sit" with your monkey may be almost impossible. Spider monkeys tend to become obsessively attached to their owners. They can suffer from severe separation anxiety. What will you do if you have to be away from your spider monkey, and what costs might be incurred relative to its care in your absence?

Chapter 5 - Daily Care of Spider Monkeys

In estimating the potential total cost of monkey ownership, err on the side of higher expenses so you are prepared for anything that might come up.

6. Example of Estimated Costs

The initial cost of a spider monkey (varies widely by breeder) is $2800 (£1,832) to $6000 (£3,028).

Sanitary supplies - depending on the monkey's age, plan on 6 to 12 diaper changes a day at a cost of $6 to $12 (£3.88 to £7.75) a day or $180 to $360 (£116.26 to £232.52) a month.

Fresh fruit and vegetables will cost $400 to $800 (£258.36 to £516.72). Depending on source and availability, this estimate could be dramatically lower.

One sack of 20 lb. of dry monkey chow will cost approximately, $45 (£29.06). (This should last 3 to 4 months.)

Leash, collar, and harness in some workable combination, $25 (£16.19) - $75 (£48.44).

Regular veterinary exams and testing $250-$300, (£164-£196).

Initial construction of habitat/enclosure including any modifications required to your primary dwelling, for instance, indoor/outdoor access for your pet monkey. $500 to $5000+ (£322.95 to £3229.50+).

Enhancement equipment including, but not limited to, swings, nets, ropes, nesting boxes, bedding and floor cover, toys, and intellectual stimulation including a television or radio will cost $750 - $2500 (£484.42 to £1614.75).

Chapter 5 - Daily Care of Spider Monkeys

On the low end of the estimated costs, to acquire a spider monkey, set up its enclosure, and secure the necessary supplies expect to spend $5000 to $12,500 (£3229.50 to £8073.75).

Once the monkey is an established member of your household, monthly expenses (in months when no veterinary care is required) should average $625 to $1000 (£403.68 to £645.90).

A Word on Expenses

Please note that all calculations here err on the side of "most expensive." Obviously anyone thinking about acquiring an exotic pet wants to know what kind of expenses they will be facing, but costs vary widely on every single item listed. It is imperative that you make a list of what your spider monkey needs and calculate the costs based on what the goods and services cost in your area, plus a consideration of how much you can do yourself.

For instance, monkey owners who have a yard full of fruit trees, who have their own garden, or who have access to a local farmer's market can immediately cut their expenses. The same is true for "do it yourself" types who can construct and design enclosures or build enrichment devices at prices far below retail with no labor costs involved.

A Word on Insurance Costs

Any consideration of monthly expenses should also include exotic pet liability insurance. Some owners, however, do not take out this extra insurance cover. Again, exact calculations are impossible to determine, as this is a "gray" area of underwriting. You must talk to an insurance professional who will likely ask to evaluate your property and the monkey's habitat before quoting a premium price.

Chapter 6 - Creating a Spider Monkey Habitat

Housing a spider monkey is not simply a matter of buying a cage and putting out some food and water. Monkeys are active, intelligent creatures that need constant stimulation if they are to exhibit normal behavior and live happily in captivity.

1. Design Considerations

The first thing you have to consider is available space, both indoors and out. A combination of the two works best, but begin with a consideration of square footage. Monkeys need room to play, climb, swing, and even hide. If you don't have enough space, a monkey may not be the right pet for you. From the beginning, you have to honestly evaluate what you can allocate for the animal's needs out of a fair consideration for its physical and emotional wellbeing.

Indoor vs. Outdoor

What is your climate? Spider monkeys come from the tropical rain forests of Central and South America. They need outdoor time. If you're in a region that gets a great deal of snow, how are you going to provide for your monkey's natural need for exercise while keeping the animal warm and comfortable?

Housing a monkey indoors at all times is challenging at best for the owner. Remember that monkeys cannot be housebroken, so sanitation is a major concern. With no interaction with a natural environment, the animal's anxiety levels may well escalate, and more intellectual stimulation will be required to prevent boredom, and outbursts.

Chapter 6 - Creating a Spider Monkey Habitat

Many monkey owners create "rooms" for their pets. While the monkey may enjoy the same kinds of toys as a human child, you are still dealing with an animal that wants to be outside and in the trees or climbing on some provided structure. A consideration of vertical space is still necessary even for an exclusively indoor monkey.

Cage vs. Natural Habitat

In the best of all worlds, a monkey in captivity would live in an environment that gave it no sense of being caged. Unfortunately, most people can't afford something so elaborate as a fully designed natural habitat, and have to do the best they can with their budget, their available space, and their imagination.

Creativity on your part is absolutely key to the health and happiness of your pet. Studies have shown that captive animals suffer high levels of stress when they have no sense of control over their lives, which is often the result of nothing to do.

Clearly, monkeys do have to be confined and controlled. They can't be allowed to run free. It isn't safe for them, or for anyone around them. With effort and creativity, however, their environment can be managed to give them the greatest sense of freedom possible under the circumstances.

When you speak in terms of "caging" a monkey, realize that a limited amount of space cannot comprise the animal's entire existence. Spider monkeys must have adequate space to exhibit natural — and thus manageable — behavior, and it is essential that they be able to climb.

Use of Vertical Space

In the wild, spider monkeys rarely come to the ground. They live almost 90 feet (27.4 meters) off of the floor of the rain forest.

They move through the trees with incredible skill and grace, making use of their limbs and tails to swing, leap, and climb.

They will even hang suspended from branches by only their tails to feed and to drink. Because their prehensile tails can extend to three feet in length, spider monkeys are really only comfortable sitting when on branches or perches where they can drape their tails out of the way.

One of the greatest mistakes owners make is neglecting to create intellectual stimulation and enrichment features high up in the enclosure. Bars and ropes for swinging, planks for climbing, sleeping and lounging platforms, the use of nets — anything that allows the spider monkey to move in the most natural fashion possible — are highly desirable and necessary components of any enclosure.

2. Intellectual Stimulation

Many owners fail to realize that building a habitat for a monkey is not just about shelter. Spider monkeys are naturally inquisitive animals, and they are highly susceptible to boredom. There are ways to alleviate this problem, including a number of methods associated with feeding activities.

Food Puzzles

Because spider monkeys are skilled foragers, they enjoy problem solving to find what they eat, which makes food puzzles well suited to distribute not only a meal, but also an engaging riddle.

To build a simple food puzzle, use a hollow tube (preferably a log or length of bamboo.) Drill holes in the sides large enough for the monkey to reach through. Make a small circular cover for each opening. Drill a hole at the top of each cover.

Use a nail slightly smaller than the hole to secure the cover in place. This will allow the monkey to push the cover aside and reach into the interior. Hang the puzzle feeders horizontally inside the enclosure, place fruit and other treats inside the tube, changing the supply daily.

A variant on this arrangement would involve using a vertical tube. Drill a series of small holes around the sides through which twigs or even dowels can be threaded. Create a larger hole at the bottom. Drop food or treats at the top of the tube. The monkeys will learn to remove the twigs or dowels until the treat falls to the bottom, where they can retrieve it.

Spider monkeys are so skillful with their hands that you can even place food inside simple translucent containers like water bottles with twist tops. In no time, the monkey will figure out how to take the lid off.

The biggest challenge is that the monkey is always going to be one step ahead of you. They may learn faster than you can create new food puzzles!

Toys

The kinds of toys you would offer a baby monkey as opposed to a full grown adult would be quite different. These bright and inquisitive creatures can be endlessly fascinated by almost anything, but it's imperative to keep their safety in mind.

You don't want them swallowing objects that would be a choking hazard, or chewing on power cords. Spider monkeys require as much or more supervision than a bright and active toddler.

As they grow, they will want heavier, more physical toys. Spider monkeys respond well to swings, jungle gyms, climbing walls, ropes, hammocks, ladders, planks, nets, and trapeze bars among others. Try to think of these features as "enrichment" as opposed

Chapter 6 - Creating a Spider Monkey Habitat

to "toys." Monkeys are active and strong. Their idea of play would be your idea of a power work out at the gym.

Sleeping Boxes

Provide a sleeping box so your spider monkey can have some privacy. Place this well above the ground. Remember that in the wild, spider monkeys sleep in the forks of branches high in the rain forest canopy. Use a sturdy wooden box, open on one side. You can line it with hay, or allow the monkey to arrange the bedding as it pleases.

Food and Fresh Water

Food hidden throughout the enclosure is one of the best enrichment devices you can offer a spider monkey. Make your monkey look for his breakfast and dinner. It's what he would do in the wild. Provide running or dripping water for the same reason.

Television and Music

Monkeys like television and music, but use these devices with care around your pet. Always place the television or radio out of reach, or in a plexiglass box. Your monkey could injure or kill himself turning over a television or chewing on the electrical cables.

2. Need for Variety

Researchers believe that the spider monkey's superior intelligence is a result of his life as a jungle forager. These animals must retain a complex store of knowledge about what they eat, as well as where to find it and when. They are acute

Chapter 6 - Creating a Spider Monkey Habitat

observers of their surroundings. Once they have learned a trick or mastered a skill, they're ready to move on to something else.

For monkey owners, this presents a unique challenge. Generally a monkey will be content with a new "toy" or "construct" for about a day, maybe two. It's important to constantly vary their sources of enrichment, removing, adding, and altering structures and elements at random, but routinely.

A bored monkey is a very, very naughty monkey. If you don't give your pet something with which to amuse himself, he will come up with a plan on his own. This usually leads to highly creative destruction.

There is an upside to this constant need for variety. Monkeys who derive interest and intellectual sustenance from their environment display fewer abnormal and aggressive behaviors and are, on a whole, much healthier.

Chapter 7 - Spider Monkey Health

Spider monkey health is absolutely dependent on a good diet, owner vigilance, and a clean, well-sanitized environment. These aspects of preventive health, along with daily inspections and annual veterinarian visits, cannot be overlooked.

1. Common Illnesses and Conditions

Sad though it may be, the reason that monkeys are used in medical research is that they suffer from many of the same conditions and diseases that plague humans. An understanding of your pet monkey's vulnerability to a range of preventable conditions, many tied to diet, is crucial in keeping the animal healthy.

Obesity, Diabetes, and Hypertension

Visitors in zoos are used to seeing signs that say, "Don't feed the animals." Some of that is for the protection of the humans, the rest is to protect the animals -- from themselves.

Spider monkeys are talented extortionists. It doesn't matter if the animal lives in a zoo enclosure or your backyard. If he can talk you out of your food, especially sweets, and unhealthy treats, he will. Monkeys that eat a diet rich in fat, sugar, and salt suffer from the same diseases that affect humans.

It's important to remember that obesity is itself a disease. It is not uncommon for over-indulged spider monkeys to weigh twice their normal size of approximately 24 lbs. (10.8 kg). These animals are prime candidates for cases of diabetes and hypertension. Of the two, diabetes is by far the most common in pet monkeys, and to some degree zoo animals.

Chapter 7 - Spider Monkey Health

The difference is that zoo animals tend to be fed a balanced diet. Additionally, they have larger, more natural enclosures and get more exercise. But even in game preserves in Asia and Africa, diabetes crops up in monkeys who are panhandling sweets from the tourists. Just like us, the monkeys lack willpower, and they suffer the dietary consequences.

Most monkeys are diagnosed with Type 2 diabetes or "adult-onset" diabetes. Overweight, pregnant females face a high risk of developing gestational diabetes, which resolves once they have given birth. For the duration of their pregnancy, however, the animal's diet must be altered if the baby is to be saved. (Type 1 diabetes is rare in spider monkeys.)

The leading risk factors for the development of diabetes in monkeys include:

- Having been raised on a bottle from infancy.
- Obesity.
- Living inside.
- Living alone or with few companions.
- A sedentary lifestyle.
- Boredom.
- The onset of middle age.
- An over-abundance of foods that are high in starch, fat, and sugar.
- Too much food on a daily basis.
- A lack of dietary fiber.

Pet monkeys should be evaluated for diabetes if they drink excessive amounts of water, indicating thirst, and if they begin to urinate frequently. Sudden weight loss and dental issues are also key warning signs.

A diabetic monkey will need to be put on a diet to normalize its weight. Steps to increase physical activity are also necessary. Oral medications or insulin injections (along with regular monitoring of blood sugar levels) will be required if the diabetes cannot be controlled by lifestyle modifications.

In cases of hypertension, the same solutions are necessary to lower blood pressure and to avoid stroke and heart attack.

Inflammatory Bowel Disease

Any time a spider monkey presents with enteritis (intestinal inflammation) accompanied by diarrhea (potentially with blood in the stool), tests should be conducted to determine that no parasites are present. If there are none, inflammatory bowel disease can be the culprit. To accurately diagnose this problem, an endoscopic examination of the intestinal tract may be required.

Controlling inflammation levels, often with the steroid prednisone, is recommended in the short term. Side effects are an issue, however, so long-term use is not recommended. Dietary changes to foods tolerated without episodes of diarrhea are the preferred solution. Non-steroidal anti-inflammatory may be used to manage minor bouts of inflammation. This is, however, a highly subjective disease, and each individual monkey will present with varying levels of sensitivity.
Although inflammatory bowel disease has clear physical components, emotional and environmental stress play a role in the severity of any outbreak. Many of the monkeys that suffer from bowel problems are heavily stressed, nervous, and hyperactive.

Tooth Removal as a Control Measure

All species of monkeys have approximately 36 teeth, including sharp and prominent canines. In an effort to control aggressive behavior and to mitigate the chance of injury, owners will sometimes ask veterinarians to remove all or part of their spider monkey's teeth. The practice is considered cruel, and it is extremely difficult to find a reputable vet who will agree to do it. The most important thing for owners to know, however, is that although the animal will not be able to bite, it can still cause a considerable amount of damage, and tooth removal will not curb its aggressive tendencies.

Mental Illness

Obviously a monkey cannot stretch out on an analyst's couch and discuss its fears and anxieties. What it can do, however, is exhibit a cascade of abnormal behaviors that range from agitated pacing and swinging to near catatonic hiding.

Spider monkeys in captivity react strongly to limited physical space. The larger the monkey's enclosure and the more intellectual enrichment it includes, the better chance the monkey will have to literally stay "sane."

Monkeys that exhibit high levels of aggression, especially unprovoked episodes of anger, are likely bored, nervous, and very lonely animals. It's important to remember that in the wild, spider monkeys are social; living in close knit bands that forage daily in cooperative and coordinated efforts.

Critics of keeping spider monkeys as pets liken having a sole monkey to putting a prisoner in solitary confinement. Great care must be taken on the part of the owner to prevent monkeys from living such a life.

That being said, it is only fair to point out that some monkeys, especially when they reach sexual maturity from age 6 to 7, never adapt to life as pets even if they are born in captivity. This raises a terrible conundrum for harassed and harried owners who simply do not know what to do with their animals.

Chapter 7 - Spider Monkey Health

Monkeys who have been raised as pets are not candidates for zoo adoption, throwing the owners on the mercy of sanctuaries and rescue groups to provide a suitable second home for their former pets. Although most of these animals will never be "normal" per se, they often improve when they are able to live with and interact with others of their own kind.

2. Disease Transmission

A primate's system so closely resembles that of man that disease transmission can travel in both directions: monkey to man and man to monkey. It's important for pet owners to understand how diseases may be transmitted to protect both themselves and their spider monkey.

Zoonotic Diseases and Transmission Routes

Zoonotic diseases originate in animals, but may be transmitted to humans. There are four major ways these diseases can be communicated.

- *Aerosol* disease transmission occurs when droplets from an infected individual are spread on the air and breathed in by the person. These droplets can be the consequence of a sneeze, fluid from birth, or a spray from urine.

- *Oral* disease transmission occurs from ingesting any food or drinking any water that has been contaminated with a potential pathogen. This includes animal products like milk and meat that have not been pasteurized or properly cooked. Oral transmission can also occur when a human handles an animal and does not wash their hands before having a meal.

- *Direct Contact* disease transmission occurs when pathogens enter open wounds, mucous membranes, or the skin.

- **Fomites** are inanimate objects that can harbor pathogens that lead to disease transmission. These might include unsterilized veterinarian implements, brushes, needles, clothing, or bedding.

Monkey to Man

The major diseases that can be spread by spider monkeys to man are herpes B, tuberculosis, and a host of conditions caused by parasites and bacteria. (These might include, but are not limited to, amoebic dysentery, salmonella, and shigella.)

Man to Monkey

The major diseases that can be spread from man to spider monkeys include colds, measles, tetanus, tuberculosis, and herpes 1 (the common virus responsible for cold sores, which can be fatal to the monkeys.)

Introducing New Monkeys to the Household

Any time a new monkey is introduced to the household, the animal should be thoroughly evaluated by a veterinary professional first, and tested for diseases, including parasitical infections.

Although spider monkeys do not regularly show aggression toward one another in the wild, it is difficult to predict how they will behave in captivity, especially if both individuals have spent the bulk of their lives alone.

Take introductions slowly, and do not leave the animals unsupervised until you are sure peaceful relations have been established.

Chapter 7 - Spider Monkey Health

Signs of Illness and Disease in Monkeys

In order to practice an effective routine of preventive care, perform daily checks of the condition of your monkey's hair and skin. Look at the animal's eyes, checking for discharge. Do the eyes look alert and interested or does the monkey have a dull gaze and seem detached? What is the animal's overall behavior? Is anything "off"? If there are other monkeys in the group, what is the level and nature of the individual's social interaction? Is he staying by himself or acting aggressively towards others? How is the animal's appetite, and are its elimination habits normal? A vet should evaluate any changes in regular behavior that go on for more than a few hours.

Finding a Vet

Veterinary care is one of the most difficult aspects of monkey ownership. It is extremely difficult to find a vet that is knowledgeable about monkey health. In the United States, owners should consult:

- Association of Primate Veterinarians at www.primatevets.org
- Monkey Zone at www.monkeyzone.com/vetzone1.htm
- Association of Exotic Mammal Veterinarians at www.aemv.org

In Great Britain, monkey owners who are having a difficult time locating a primate veterinarian should contact the Primate Society of Great Britain at www.psgb.com.

Routine Veterinary Testing

On an annual basis, a veterinarian professional should examine the monkey. Records should be maintained about vital signs to detect changes over time, for instance the development and progression of a heart murmur. The vet should thoroughly examine the animal's eyes and ears, its external features, and the teeth. Note that these procedures will likely have to be performed with the animal sedated.

Fecal testing for parasites should be conducted biannually, with annual blood testing and a screening for tuberculosis.

Vaccinations

Vaccinations are an accepted part of pet ownership. The shots are intended to prevent the animal from contracting diseases, some of which, like rabies, can be transmitted to humans.

Monkey owners should be aware that there are no approved vaccines for use with small primates. If you have your pet vaccinated, the use of the vaccines will be "off label."

This is not to say that the vaccines will not function properly, but they will be formulated for human children, not for monkeys. Adverse side effects can occur, ranging from mild skin irritation and a low-grade fever to life-threatening allergic reactions.

Typically, when pet monkeys are vaccinated, the shots are to protect them from measles, tetanus, and rabies. Scheduled booster shots may be required for full protection.

Most primate vets recommend the following schedule for monkey vaccinations:

- measles and tetanus at 7 months
- measles, tetanus, and rabies at 14 months
- rabies booster annually
- tetanus shot every 5 to 7 years

The most common side effects seen within four to 12 hours of the vaccination are a low-grade fever, lethargy, a loss of appetite, and irritability. These problems should resolve in 24 to 72 hours. If they persist after three days, the animal should be taken back to the vet clinic for evaluation.

Reactions at the site of the shot may include swelling, hives, or redness. If the monkey shows any signs of respiratory distress, immediately return to the vet clinic to seek emergency aid.

Locating a Primate Vet

One of the biggest hurdles faced by monkey owners is simply finding a vet who will care for their pet. Most vets at regular small animal hospitals will not treat monkeys not only because they do not have expertise with the species, but because they are concerned about liability issues.

Be prepared to have to travel to find a primate vet, which raises issues of transport and potentially overnight lodging. Educate yourself about first aid measures that may have to be taken with your pet if you live at a considerable distance from a primate vet. If your monkey requires any kind of ongoing treatments, like the administration of shots or fluids, you will have to ask to be trained in performing these tasks.

The Cost of Medical Care

It is impossible to guess what medical care for your monkey will cost. Much of the issue may revolve around your proximity to the vet, and how much you have to spend on travel to find care services for your pet.

From there, prices depend entirely on what your animal needs in terms of procedures, tests, and medications.

For a regular exam and routine testing, expect to pay at least $250 to $300 (£164-£196), although your costs may be

Chapter 7 - Spider Monkey Health

considerably more. Obviously, if you are looking at any kind of surgical procedure, the bills will mount exponentially.

Chapter 8 - Spider Monkey Reproduction

There is no specific breeding period for spider monkeys, although mating intensifies from November to February, coinciding with the wet season in the rain forest. Sexual maturity varies slightly by species. Males normally reach adulthood at age 5 and females at age 4. (In some species of spider monkeys, sexual maturity is not attained until age 6 and 7 respectively.)

Female spider monkeys have an estrus cycle of 24 to 27 days, followed by 2 to 3 days of sexual receptivity. Individual females give birth every 2 to 4 years. The single births occur after a gestation period of 226-232 days.

1. Courtship

Female monkeys are in charge of the courtship ritual. Although both males and females engage in anogenital sniffing to verify their potential partner's readiness to mate, the final choice is made by the female.

When the female has made her choice, she presents her genitals to the selected male. If he indicates that he is interested, the two will separate from the group for a period of hours or days.

2. Infant Care

Most spider monkey infants are born black, and attain their adult coloration sometime after they stop nursing at age two. For the first five months of the infant's life, the mother carries the baby everywhere.

Infants are completely dependent on their mothers for a period of 10 to 12 weeks, after which the young spider monkeys begin to explore and play on their own with other youngsters. The babies ride on their mother's backs for at least a year, and often females will form living bridges with their bodies and tails to help young monkeys get across dangerous stretches of the forest canopy.

Young spider monkeys stay close to their mothers for four years, even if the female has given birth to another infant in that period of time. Male spider monkeys have no role in the rearing of their offspring.

3. Death of an Infant

The interval between births for females depends entirely on the survival of their offspring. If the infant lives, the mother will care for the infant until it is completely weaned, which can take as much as four years.

If, however, the infant does not survive, or is taken from the mother, the female will resume estrus and reproduce as soon as she is once again receptive to the attentions of a male.

Scientists have observed that the higher-ranking females in spider monkey bands tend to give birth more often, with lower ranking females experiencing longer gaps between pregnancies.

4. Breeding in Captivity

Any person wanting to breed and sell spider monkeys (or to exhibit or perform research with the animals) must be licensed by the U.S. Department of Agriculture in the United States and hold a Dangerous Wild Animal license in the U.K.

Do not buy a monkey from any source other than an approved breeder who can produce evidence of accreditation. Such facilities are subject to inspection and are legally bound to provide a degree of veterinary care for their animals.

Chapter 8 - Spider Monkey Reproduction

There is also a substantially lessened chance of acquiring an inbred animal from a legally accredited dealer. Zoos in the United States that are members of the Association of Zoos and Aquariums develop Species Survival Plans that allow them to maintain the genetic vigor of their captive populations by matching breeding pairs across locations.

Private breeders who are not reputable are just as capable of running a "mill" operation, as is often the case with purebred puppies and kittens. Because spider monkeys are at their most adorable and "adoptable" status as tiny infants, dealers who see only the profit potential of the animals take them from their mothers at far too young an age and put them into the marketplace for adoption.

Not only is this process traumatic for the infants, but also it is terrible for the mothers who share a deep bond with their offspring. Single spider monkeys living in captivity often experience separation anxiety, and baby monkeys who have not received adequate maternal care are even more likely to develop abnormal psychological reactions.

When you are looking for a spider monkey from a breeder, be aware of these factors and find out as much as you can about the facility before agreeing to adopt one of their animals. How the monkeys are housed, the degree of socialization they receive when they are young, and the vigor of the available gene pool are all important factors in producing an animal with a greater chance of adapting to life as a pet.

Private Breeding of Spider Monkeys is Discouraged

In most cases, spider monkey ownership is limited to one animal at a time. Some people who live in the country, or who have adequate backyard space and generous local zoning laws can get away with having multiple monkey pets, but that is a rare situation.

Chapter 8 - Spider Monkey Reproduction

People who are desirous of breeding spider monkeys (usually for profit) require special licensing in both the United States and the United Kingdom. Spider monkeys are capable of breeding year round, and mothers whose babies are taken away from them will resume their cycles immediately.

Breeding captive monkeys is, however, a highly specialized business involving not just medical issues, but also matters of genetics to maintain a vigorous and healthy population. It is not recommended that owners attempt to breed their monkeys without professional assistance.

Spider monkeys become aggressive once they have reached sexual maturity, and can be much more difficult to handle during those periods of time when their hormones are surging.

In many cases, breeders will only offer animals for sale that have been spayed or neutered.

Chapter 9 - Spider Monkey Resources

The Internet has become a prime source of information for all exotic pet owners. In the 21st century, we believe that we can "Google" anything. Be warned, however, that if you search online for the phrase "spider monkey forums," you will likely find a lot of information about SpiderMonkey, which was the first JavaScript engine written by Brendan Eich of Netscape in the fall of 1996.

The code was subsequently released as open source and is now maintained by the Mozilla Foundation and is used for support functions for Firefox and the GNOME 3 desktop. Consequently, there are a lot of computer forums dedicated to the discussion of "SpiderMonkey."

If you are looking for information regarding your pet spider monkey include the words "exotic animal" or similar qualifiers to refine your search results.

1. Reference Websites and Materials

There are many good websites with information on spider monkeys in the wild and in captivity. These include, but are not limited to:

Net at pin.primate.wisc.edu

This is the Library and Information Service maintained by the National Primate Research Center at the University of Wisconsin - Madison. The information covers a wide variety of primates including spider monkeys

2nd Chance
Although this website can be a little challenging to navigate, the All Creature Care section at www.2ndchance.info/ACC.htm

Chapter 9 - Spider Monkey Resources

allows users to search the available articles for the word "monkey."

A number of useful pieces come up, including:

- "Pet Monkeys - What About Keeping Monkeys as Pets?"
- "Dealing with Fat Monkeys - Obesity in Pet and Captive Monkeys"
- "Diabetes in Your Pet Monkey - Why It Happened, What You Need to Do"
- "Vaccination of Exotic Pets and Wild Animals"
- "Diseases We Catch from Our Pets"
- "Animal Environmental Enrichment"

Pet Monkey Info at www.petmonkeyinfo.com

Although some of the information on this site in regard to legal issues affecting primate ownership is dated, there is still a wealth of information on care tips, cages, and enrichment as well as the excellent article, "So, You Think You Want a Monkey!"

Pet Monkey at www.petmonkey.info

This is a straightforward resource for prospective owners still on the fence about deciding whether or not they want to or can welcome a spider monkey into their home. The sections include:

- Advantages of Monkeys as Pets
- Disadvantages of Monkeys as Pets
- Monkeys as Surrogate Children
- Why We Believe Monkeys are Not Pets
- Laws Regarding Pet Monkeys

About.com Exotic Pets
The Problem with Pet Monkeys at
http://exoticpets.about.com/cs/primates/a/primatesaspets.htm

A good overview piece addressing the commitment required of monkey owners, this text also tackles the major hurdles including aggression, housing, and the mess. (Note that at the bottom of this article there are suggested readings and related articles.)

A Note About Online Research

Be forewarned that when you begin to research spider monkey ownership online, you will encounter many cautionary pages and outright negative commentary. Don't dismiss those pages as just animal rights activists ranting.

Read the good, the bad, and the ugly about having a monkey as a pet. No one should ever adopt a monkey without all the information. Anything less would be an injustice to you, your family, and the animal.

No matter how much you may want a pet monkey, or how outstandingly you intend to care for it, there are compelling reasons not to keep monkeys as pets. As part of the process of deciding whether a pet monkey is for you, that material should also be considered.

2. Supplies and Equipment

Monkey owners are forced, by the very exotic nature of their primate companions, to be "do it yourself" types, especially when it comes to building enclosures and designing enrichment elements. There are, however, some online sources for a range of monkey-related items, including sanitary supplies and even clothing. Some to consider include:

- Pampered Primates and K9s at www.pamperedprimatesandk9s.com
- Primatestore at www.primatestore.com
- Monkey Needs at www.monkeyneeds.com
- Jeffers Pet at www.jefferspet.com
- Exotic Nutrition at www.exoticnutrition.com

- Animal World Network at
www.animalworldnetwork.com/primates.html
- Monkey Cages 4 Less at www.monkeycages4less.com

Note on Searching Online for Supplies

When searching online for supplies, don't limit your search term to "spider monkeys." Search for "primate supplies" and "exotic pet supplies." Many of the links above are to online pet "malls" that have primate sections. There are many smaller "boutique" sites, some even offering handmade items for pet monkeys.

3. Support and Discussion Groups

Owners of pet spider monkeys are always hungry for information and new ideas. Like many specialized communities, these people have found a place to gather online to exchange information and to support one another in this sometimes-difficult proposition of keeping a primate. Some good sources include:

- Primates Pal at www.primatepal.com
- Exotic Pets Community at
http://www.medhelp.org/forums/Exotic-Pets/show/5?page=2
- Monkey Kisses at www.monkeykisses.com

Chapter 10 - Conclusion

With everything you have now learned about spider monkeys in the wild and in captivity, you may be debating back and forth about whether or not to bring one of these delightful but challenging primates into your life. No one can make that decision for you, but out of this lengthy discussion, the following are some salient points to consider.
Remember, a spider monkey is NOT a pet and they belong in the wild but if you DO decide to get one, regardless, look after it as good as you possibly can and give the monkey a good home, although, of course, their home is in the wild.

1. The Blessing and the Problem of Monkey Longevity

From the beginning, realize that adopting a spider monkey represents a greater commitment than bringing home a puppy or a kitten. Your monkey may live 40 years. This is the same kind of blessing and problem encountered by people who own parrots, some of which live past age 75.

Oddly, both monkeys and parrots develop equally deep and intimate bonds with their owners. Both animals are highly intelligent and capable of storing up a lifetime of experiences that shape their behavior and feelings; and they are capable of experiencing grief. What will happen to your monkey if you die? Are you prepared to make provisions for your monkey in your will and to leave money to ensure the animal's standard of care is maintained?

2. Forget the Myth of the Dumb Animal

Spider monkeys are one of the most intelligent of all primates. Your monkey will need more from you than food and shelter. He

Chapter 10 - Conclusion

will require your attention and time, and your creative interaction. This is actually the reason many people adopt monkeys. Their sharp intellect and capacity to amass a vocabulary on par with a four-year-old child makes them more friend and companion than pet.

That being said, you will have a responsibility to feed your monkey's intellectual appetite as well as his body's need for nutrition. This means constantly varying your monkey's environment, providing a habitat that accommodates his need for physical activity, and feeding him in ways that fulfill his need to forage.

You could even find yourself buying a TV to be placed adjacent to your monkey's enclosure, and shopping for DVDs he would like. Monkeys learn from what goes on around them. Your pet will learn to recognize and like things in your world -- and potentially dislike others.

3. Monkeys Don't Always React Well to Strangers

Monkey owners report that their pets often react poorly when new people come into their owner's lives. This can be a huge challenge if your monkey takes an instant dislike to someone you like or even love. It's one thing for your cat not to like your new boyfriend, but your monkey can and will exhibit real and active jealousy.

When you adopt your monkey, immediately begin to socialize the animal to the people in your life that the monkey will see on a regular basis. If you do bring someone new into your life, introduce that person to the monkey slowly and cautiously. You especially want to avoid a situation where the monkey becomes aggressive to the point of biting.

4. Monkeys Are Expensive Pets

When prospective monkey owners think about expense, they usually don't go much farther than the cost of the animal itself. Don't fall into that trap. Chapter 5 of this book attempts to run down a monkey's daily needs and to provide a basis for projecting a wide range of associated costs.

It is important to remember that some of these expenses are "one time" or "set up" costs, but to truly keep your monkey happy, the animal will need a constant supply of fresh fruits and vegetables. While it is not necessary to buy organic produce for your pet, the fresher the food, the better. Many of the health problems pet spider monkeys experience are diet related, including digestive issues.

5. Health Care for Your Monkey May Be a Challenge

Not all vets are willing or able to treat primate patients. Monkeys need annual exams, vaccinations, and blood and fecal tests. They are susceptible to many of the same conditions that plague humans including diabetes and hypertension.

When you do find a good primate vet, you may be forced to travel some distance to get your pet the care it needs to stay in optimal health. It may be a good idea to investigate primate veterinarian care available in your area before you adopt your monkey and to get projected annual costs to help you with your adoption decision.

6. Making the Decision to Adopt

When you have weighed all the positive and negative factors associated with adopting a spider monkey, and made the decision to go forward, prepare the people in your life. Don't be surprised

Chapter 10 - Conclusion

if your friends and family are taken aback by your plans, or if they express fear about the monkey.

When spider monkeys are young babies, they are completely docile and dependent on their keepers. Basically, you are about to become a "parent." The chances are high that it will be your monkey who is more scared than anyone.

Introduce the animal to your friends and family slowly, encouraging other people to be as calm and gentle around the monkey as they would be around a tiny infant. Spider monkey babies are captivatingly sweet. It won't be long before your new pet has won the hearts of all the people that will be a part of its life.

7. Prepare Everything in Advance

Have everything you need to care for your spider monkey in place before you bring the animal home - including its enclosure complete with enrichment features. Remember, the monkey will need to acclimate itself to the world the two of you will share. Your job is to create a sense of safety and security for your pet. This feeling will only grow as your monkey gets to know you and bond with you.

Plan on having lots of time to spend with your monkey, especially in the beginning. In the wild, spider monkey babies are completely dependent on their mothers for the first year, and stay close to them for up to four years. That level of dependence will be transferred to you.

There are many cautionary tales about monkeys that have literally gone mad from the boredom and loneliness of captivity. This does not and should not be how your relationship with your spider monkey turns out. The fact that you have spent your time reading this text and learning about monkeys and their needs shows your desire to care for your new pet properly.

Chapter 10 - Conclusion

Monkeys, like humans, will respond to kindness, loving attention, and companionship. A spider monkey can be a beguiling companion, part trickster and part playmate, he will make you laugh, amaze you with his ability to learn and to interact, and move you with his affection and loyalty.

If you are ready to welcome a spider monkey into your home and heart, do so with both a sense of responsibility and love. You're in for a rewarding adventure that will give you keen insight into the mind of an animal that will be far more like you than you realize. Spider monkeys never fail to intrigue and delight. Simply put, there's no other pet quite like one of these intelligent, agile, and lovable primates.

Glossary

agoutis - A large burrowing rodent with long legs native to Central America and related to the guinea pig.

alloparenting - A term used in biology and sociology describing a situation in which individuals, other than the parents, act in a parental capacity.

ape - Apes are large primates. They do not have tails and their nostrils point forward. Apes include gorillas, chimpanzees, orangutans, and gibbons.

arboreal - relating to trees or to animals that live chiefly in trees.

ateles - The genus of spider monkeys in scientific nomenclature.

brachiation - A method of movement practiced by monkeys in which they use their arms to swing rhythmically from branch to branch.

bridging - In relation to spider monkeys, this refers to the behavior of a group of females who use their bodies and prehensile tails to form living bridges to allow young, weaker infants to cross distances safely in the rain forest canopy.

canopy - Refers to the upper tree levels of the Central and South American rain forest.

catarrhines - Refers to the group of Old World monkeys, apes, and humans.

deforestation - The destructive process by which the Central and South American rain forests are being cleared of trees.

dichromatic - In terms of vision, the ability to see only two colors.

Glossary

diurnal - Refers to animals active during the daylight hours.

domesticated - Animals that have been tamed to work for or live with humans.

DWAA - Acronym for the principle U.K. law governing the owning of wild animals including primates, the Dangerous Wild Animals Act of 1976.

ecosystem - In biology, an ecosystem in an interactive community of organisms and their relationship to their physical environment.

enrichment - In reference to spider monkeys, this term refers to any strategy or device intended to create intellectual stimulation or to make the animal's environment more challenging and interesting to combat boredom.

fission-fusion - Refers to a type of social organization in which a community breaks into smaller groups for a specific purpose and then reassembles.

fomites - An inanimate object from which an infectious disease is transmitted.

food puzzle - In reference to spider monkeys, any means of feeding the animal that forces the monkey to solve a puzzle to acquire a treat or meal, thus appealing to its native food foraging instincts.

foraging - The acquisition of food by some process of hunting, which may refer to the gathering of plant matter.

friction pad - Refers to a strip of bare skin on the underside of the tip of a spider monkey's tail. Resembling a fingerprint, this patch is useful in the tail's ability to grasp and hold on to objects.

frugivorous - Consuming a diet made up primarily of fruit.

Glossary

hypertension - The medical term for high blood pressure.

indigenous - Native to or naturally occurring in a given area.

intellectual stimulation - In reference to spider monkeys, any strategy or device used to enhance the animal's environment for the purpose of decreasing boredom.

IUCN - The International Union for the Conservation of Nature, the group responsible for maintaining the "Red List" of vulnerable, threatened, endangered, and critically endangered species.

monkey - Small to medium-sized monkeys that have tails, snouts, and nostrils that point to the side.

natal - Referring or relating to the place of a person or animal's birth. In the case of spider monkeys, most commonly refers to the habit of males of staying with the group into which they were born. Females tend to migrate to other groups.

New World monkey - Monkeys that are primarily indigenous to Central and South America, that have snouts, nostrils that face to the side, and prehensile tails.

nocturnal - Describes any animal that is active primarily at night.

off-display - The time in a zoo when animals cannot be seen by visitors.

Old World monkey - Monkeys that are indigenous to Asia and Africa. They do not have prehensile tails, and their nostrils are more closely spaced than those of their New World counterparts.

on-display - The time in a zoo when animals can be seen by visitors.

Glossary

parasitic disease - Any one of a number of infectious diseases transmitted by parasites.

platyrrhines - Of or pertaining to a group of New World monkeys with broad, flat noses and long, prehensile tails.

predation - The act of one animal preying upon another.

prehensile - A tail capable of grasping.

primate - The scientific order of a group of mammals including humans, apes, monkeys, marmosets, tarsiers, bush babies, and lemurs.

prosimian - A primitive group of primates in the suborder Prosimii that are considered less developed.

quadrupedal - Having four feet or moving in a manner employing all four limbs.

Red List - The list of vulnerable, threatened, endangered, and critically endangered species maintained by the International Union for the Conservation of Nature (IUCN).

sedentary - Refers to an animal or person that spends too much of its time seated or inactive.

separation anxiety - Anxiety resulting from the separation of a child from its mother, an animal from its owner, or any similar situation.

Species Survival Plan - A plan developed by member institutions of the U.S. Association of Zoos and Aquariums to more effectively breed captive animals for the health of the available gene pool and survival of the species.

suspensory - Any behavior involving suspension. In the case of spider monkeys, it refers to their habit of hanging suspended by their tails to eat or drink.

Glossary

terrestrial - An inhabitant of the earth, or an animal that lives primarily on the ground and that does not venture into the trees.

trichromatic - The ability to see three colors.

vertical space - In reference to spider monkeys, this phrase describes the amount of room available to the animal for climbing and swinging.

zoologist - A biologist specializing in the study of animals.

zoonotic - Referring to an infectious disease that can be transmitted from an animal to a human.

Appendix I

Appendix I - Pet Monkey Regulations

In both the United States and the United Kingdom it is best to adapt a "drill down" approach to determining the legality of pet monkey ownership.

In the U.S., there is no federal prohibition to owning a monkey, but state laws may prohibit primates as pets — or country — or local — or even homeowners association by-laws.

Investigate every level of regulation that might apply to owning a pet spider monkey BEFORE you acquire the animal.

U.S. Regulations Regarding Spider Monkeys by State- correct at time of printing.

Alabama
No Regulation

Alaska
Banned

Arizona
Anyone who already owns a spider monkey and who is moving to the state of Arizona must obtain a wildlife holding permit from the Department of Fish and Game. Current citizens of the state are not allowed to keep wildlife as "pets" unless they qualify for a permit. Restricted wildlife includes orangutans, chimpanzees, and gorillas, but all other non-infant primates are allowed as long as they are free of zoonotic diseases.

Arkansas
No Regulation

California

Appendix I

Banned

Colorado
Banned

Connecticut
Banned

Delaware
Permit Required

Florida
Permit Required

Georgia
Banned

Hawaii
Banned

Idaho
No Regulation

Illinois
Anyone who lawfully owned a primate before January 1, 2011 may continue to do so if the animal was registered with local wildlife control before April 1, 2011. The law specifically reads that, "No person may harbor, care for, act as a custodian, or maintain in his possession any dangerous animal or primate except at a properly maintained zoological park, federally licensed exhibit, circus, scientific institution, research laboratory, veterinary hospital or animal refuge." Spider monkeys are not specifically designated as "dangerous animals," but anyone wanting to purchase one should take the matter up first with the Illinois Department of Natural Resources.

Appendix I

Indiana
Permit Required

Iowa
Banned

Kansas
No Regulation

Kentucky / Luoisiana
Banned

Maine
Permit Required

Maryland
Banned

Massachusetts
Banned

Michigan
Michigan state law does not specifically prohibit owning a spider monkey, but the Department of Natural Resources may require any exotic animal entering the state to be examined by a veterinarian. Additionally, owners may be required to prove the animal will be properly housed, cared for, and appropriately confined.

Minnesota
Banned

Mississippi
Permit Required

Missouri

Appendix I

Permit Required

Montana
Permit Required

Nebraska
No Regulation

Nevada
No Regulation

New Hampshire
Banned

New Jersey
Banned

New Mexico
Banned

New York
Banned

North Carolina
No Regulation

North Dakota
Permit Required

Ohio
No Regulation

Oklahoma
Permit Required

Oregon
Banned

Appendix I

Pennsylvania
Permit Required

Rhode Island
Permit Required

South Carolina
No Regulation

South Dakota
Permit Required

Tennessee
While some "Class I" wildlife is prohibited in Tennessee, including gorillas, orangutans, chimpanzees, gibbons, siamangs, mandrills, drills, baboons, and Gelada baboons, the state does not regulate the private possession of monkeys.

Texas
Permit Required

Utah
Banned

Vermont
Banned

Virginia
No Regulation

Washington
Banned

West Virginia
No Regulation

Wisconsin

Appendix I

No Regulation

Wyoming
Banned

U.K. Regulations Regarding Spider Monkeys

In the U.K., a Dangerous Wild Animals (D.W.A.) license allows owners to keep primates, but certain criteria enforced by the local council must be met. Only then can an application be completed to secure the license. The rules, requirements, and regulations for obtaining and maintaining the license vary by location.

Applicants must meet specific age requirements, legally own the animal, and not have been previously prevented from obtaining a D.W.A. license due to a disqualification. It is important to verify that you have the correct amount of space and the right facilities to house a monkey.

Other considerations including financially supporting the animal throughout its life, and appropriately disposing of waste materials. Applicants may be required to have both the animal and their home inspected by a veterinarian surgeon.

Note that several weeks may be required for processing of the D.W.A. license.

Sources and Citations

http://www.northdevon.gov.uk/nonlgcl_dangerous_wild_animals
http://en.wikipedia.org/wiki/Dangerous_Wild_Animals_Act_1976
http://www.direct.gov.uk/en/Dl1/Directories/Localcouncils/index.htm

Appendix II - Primate Sanctuaries

U.S.

International Primate Protection League at www.ippl.org

Born Free USA Primate Sanctuary at www.bornfreeusa.org

Jungle Friends Primate Sanctuary at www.junglefriends.org

New England Primate Conservancy at www.neprimateconservancy.org

Mindy's Memory at www.mindysmem.org

Mostly Monkeys at www.mostlymonkeys.org

Suncoast Primate Sanctuary Foundation, Inc. at suncoastprimate.homestead.com

OPR Coastal Primate Sanctuary
http://www.oregonprimaterescue.com/

Pacific Primate Sanctuary, Inc. at www.pacificprimate.org

Primarily Primates in San Antonio, TX at http://www.primarilyprimates.org/

U.K.

Monkey Forest at www.trenthman-monkey-forest.com

Primate Society of Great Britain at www.psgb.org

The Monkey Sanctuary in Cornwall

Appendix II

(Only Global Federation of Animal Sanctuaries certified primate sanctuary in Europe.)
Monkey World at monkeyworld.org

Lakeview Monkey Sanctuary – Berkshire UK
http://www.lakeviewmonkeysanctuary.co.uk/

Wales Ape and Monkey Sanctuary
http://www.ape-monkey-rescue.org.uk/

Works Cited

"Are You Sure You Want a Monkey?" Monkey Matters Magazine as reprinted at Primate Info Net. http://pin.primate.wisc.edu/aboutp/pets/areyousure.html (Accessed 12 February 2013).

Broekema, Iris. "Natural History of the Black-Handed Spider Monkey (Ateles geoffroyi)." NurtureNatural.org. November 2002. http://www.nurturenatural.org/monkeysofpanama/spiderblack.htm (Accessed May 2013).

Cant, J.G.H. "Feeding Ecology of Spider Monkeys." Human Evolution, 1990: 5 (3), 269-281.

Captive Wild Animal Protection Coalition. "Small Monkey Fact Sheet." http://www.cwapc.org/education/download/SmallMonkeyFacts.pdf (Accessed January 2013).

Cawthon, Lang KA. 2007 April 10. Primate Factsheets: Black spider monkey (Ateles paniscus) Behavior. http://pin.primate.wisc.edu/factsheets/entry/black_spider_monkey/behav (Accessed 9 April 2013 April).

Chapman, Colin A. and Daniel M. Weary, "Variability in Spider Monkeys' Vocalizations May Provide Basis for Individual Recognition." American Journal of Primatology (1990) 22: 279-284.

Chapman, Colin A. "Primate Seed Dispersal: The Fate of Dispersed Seeds." Biotropica, 1989: 2, 148-154.

Davis, Nicolas. "Social and Environmental Influences on the Welfare of Zoo-Based Spider Monkeys (Ateles geoffroyi rufiventris). Doctoral Dissertation. University of Liverpool

Works Cited

(University of Chester), 2009. http://chesterrep.openrepository.com/cdr/handle/10034/118072 (Accessed April 2013).

Department for Environment Food and Rural Affairs (UK), "Code of Practice for the Welfare of Privately Kept Non-Human Primates," January 2010, http://archive.defra.gov.uk/wildlife-pets/pets/cruelty/documents/primate-cop.pdf (Accessed February 2013).

Duarte-Quiroga, A. and A. Estrada. "Primates as Pets in Mexico City: An Assessment of the Species Involved, Source of Origin, and General Aspects of Treatment." American Journal of Primatology, 2003 (61), 53-60.

Hines, Ron, DVM, PhD. "Are There Any Diseases My Family or I Can Catch From Pet Monkeys? Monkey Bites and Exposure." 2ndChance.info. http://www.2ndchance.info/mnky2man.htm (Accessed 5 May 2013).

Hines, Ron, DVM, PhD. "Obesity in Pet & Captive Monkeys: Fat Monkeys, Why It Happens, What You Need to Do About It." 2ndChance.info. http://www.2ndchance.info/Chubbymonkey.htm (Accessed February 2013).

Hines, Ron, DVM, PhD. "Diabetes in Your Pet Monkey: Why It Happens in Captive Monkeys, What You Need to Do." 2ndChance.info http://www.2ndchance.info/monkdiabetes.htm (Accessed January 2013).

Isaza, Ramiro, DVM; Barbara Baker, DVM; Freeland Dunker, DVM. "Medical Management of Inflammatory Bowel Disease in a Spider Monkey." Journal of the American Veterinary Medical Association. 1994. As reprinted at http://www.monkeyzone.com/medical_spider_monkey.htm (Accessed April 2013).

Works Cited

Lang, Kristina Cawthon. "Primate Factsheets: Black Spider Monkey (Ateles paniscus) Behavior." Primate Info Net. 10 April 2007. http://pin.primate.wisc.edu/factsheets/entry/black_spider_monkey/behav (Accessed 23 April 2013).

Mott, Maryann. "The Perils of Keeping Monkeys as Pets." National Geographic News, 16 September 2003. http://news.nationalgeographic.com/news/2003/09/0916_030916_primatepets.html (Accessed April 2013).

"Primate Color Vision." Primates: The Taxonomy and General Characteristics of Prosimians, Monkeys, Apes, and Humans. http://anthro.palomar.edu/primate/color.htm (Accessed April 2013).

Ramos-Fernandez, G. "Vocal Communication in a Fission-Fusion Society: Do Spider Monkeys Stay in Touch with Close Associates?" International Journal of Primatology, 2004 (26), 5: 1077-1092.

Schaffner, C.M. and Aureli, F. 2005. "Embraces and Grooming in Captive Spider Monkeys." International Journal of Primatology, 26(5), 1093-1106.

U.S. Department of Agriculture. "Licensing and Registration Under the Animal Welfare Act: Guidelines for Dealers, Exhibitors, Transporters, and Researchers." http://www.aphis.usda.gov/animal_welfare/downloads/aw/awlicreg.pdf (Accessed March 2013).

Vaughan, Adam. "Amazon Deforestation Falls Again." 3 August 2012. The Guardian. http://www.guardian.co.uk/environment/2012/aug/03/amazon-deforestation-falls-again (Accessed April 2013).

Index

Adopting a Spider Monkey, 31
adoption, 44, 72, 80, 88
Africa, 11, 12, 69
aggression, 14, 21, 34, 35, 44, 46, 57, 71, 73, 84
aggressive, 12, 25, 26, 27, 31, 34, 45, 51, 56, 59, 67, 70
Alexander von Humboldt, 20
alfalfa, 51
alloparenting, 26
Amazon, 19, 107
anxiety, 21, 25, 26, 33, 46, 59, 62, 80
Aotidae, 12
apes, 11
Appendix I, 96
arboreal, 12, 45
Asia, 11, 12, 69
Ateles, 13, 19, 20, 21, 28, 104, 106, 107
Ateles belzebuth, 19
Ateles fusciceps fusciceps, 20
Ateles fusciceps rufiventris, 20
Ateles geoffroyi geoffroyi, 21
Ateles geoffroyi ornatus, 21
Ateles geoffroyi vellerosus, 21
Ateles geoffroyi yucatanensis, 21
Ateles paniscus, 19
Atelidae, 12, 13
Atelines, 13
attachment, 33, 53
baboons, 12
bacteria, 37, 73
band alpha, 22
bands, 14, 21, 22, 23, 24, 26, 71, 79
behavioral patterns, 24

biting, 34, 40, 58, 87
Black-headed spider monkey, 20
bonobos, 11
Boredom, 46, 69
brachiation, 17
Brazil, 13, 19, 20, 27
breeders, 39, 80, 81
Brown spider monkey, 20
bushbabies, 12
Callitrichidae, 12
canopy, 13, 15, 16, 17, 18, 45, 66, 79
Captivity, 24, 25, 79
capuchins, 12
caretaker, 57
Carl Lennaeus, 19
catarrhines, 11
Cebidae, 12
Centers for Disease Control, 39, 41
Central America, 11, 21
chimpanzees, 11, 15
choking hazard, 65
clothing, 36, 73, 84
collar, 55
colobus monkeys, 12
Color Vision, 17, 106
Columbia, 19, 20, 21
commercial feeder products, 24
companionship, 26
complex commands, 38
conservation, 19, 24, 28
Cost, 44, 76
costs, 44, 50, 59, 61, 76, 88
Courtship, 78
damage, 28, 40, 71

Index

Dangerous Wild Animals Act (DWAA) 1976, 42
Death of an Infant, 79
Deforestation, 13, 28, 107
dependence, 31, 33, 34
Design Considerations, 62
diabetes, 39, 51, 52, 68, 69, 70
diapers, 31, 35, 36
Diet and Nutrition, 48
digestive issues, 88
Disease Transmission, 72
Diurnal, 18
Diurnal Foragers, 18
documentation, 43, 44
domesticated, 31, 32, 33, 92
dominant monkey, 22
ecosystem, 13
Ecuador, 19, 29
endangered, 15, 19, 20, 21, 27, 29
Enrichment, 53
Environment, 24, 105
Étienne Geoffroy Saint-Hilaire, 19, 20
exotic pet insurance, 40
Fission-Fusion, 22, 106
Flea Treatment, 58
fleas, 55, 58
flooring material, 37
Fomites, 73
Food Preparation, 49
Food Puzzles, 64
Foods to Avoid, 51
foraging parties, 22
frugivorous, 13
Fruits, 48
Geoffroy's spider monkey, 20, 21
gibbons, 11
Glossary, 91
gorillas, 11, 15
grief, 86
Group Dynamics, 22
Guiana spider monkey, 19
harness, 56, 59
Health Care, 88
Henirich Kuhl, 21
hinged thumbs, 12
hives, 76
Homeowner's Association (HOA), 40
howler, 12
humans, 12, 16, 21, 25, 26, 27, 32, 51, 55, 68, 72
Hypertension, 68
indigenous, 11, 19, 20, 21
Indoor vs. Outdoor, 62
Infant Care, 78
infant wipes, 36
Inflammatory Bowel Disease, 70, 105
insurance, 40, 41, 42, 59
insurance agent, 40
Insurance coverage, 41
Intellectual Stimulation, 53, 64
intelligence, 23, 38, 45, 47, 66
Intelligence, 15
International Union for the Conservation of Nature (IUCN), 27
Introducing New Monkeys to the Household, 73
irritability, 75
IUCN Red List of Threatened Species, 19, 28
John Edward Gray, 20
language, 37
lawsuit, 41
Legal Restrictions, 39
lethargy, 75
Licensed Breeder or Dealer, 41
licensing, 42

109

Index

Life Span, 15
Locomotion, 17
lonely, 34, 71
long-haired spider monkey, 19
long-range calls, 16, 22
lorises, 12
loss of appetite, 75
low-grade fever, 75
macaques, 12
malaria, 15
Man to Monkey, 73
marmosets, 12
measles, 73, 75
Medical Care, 76
Mental Illness, 71
mental stress, 43
Mexican spider monkey, 21
Mexico, 11, 13, 21, 27, 29, 99, 105
mobility impairments, 38
monkey sanctuaries, 26
monkeys, 11, 12, 13, 14, 15, 16, 17, 18, 19, 20, 21, 22, 23, 24, 25, 26, 27, 28, 29, 30, 31, 32, 33, 34, 35, 41, 42, 44, 45, 46, 47, 48, 50, 51, 52, 53, 54, 55, 56, 62, 63, 64, 65, 66, 68, 69, 70, 71, 73, 74, 76, 78, 79, 80
Natural Habitat, 13, 63
Nature and Culture International, 29
neutered, 81
New World monkeys, 11, 12, 15
Newspaper Classifieds, 42
Nicaraguan spider monkey, 21
nocturnal, 12
Non-human primates, 11
Nutritional Guidance, 52
Obesity, 51, 68, 69, 105

off display, 24
offspring, 15, 17, 79, 80
Old World" species, 11
opposable thumbs, 12, 45
orangutans, 11, 15
organic produce, 88
Ornate spider monkey, 21
outdoor exhibits, 24
parasites, 37, 43, 45, 70, 73, 75, 94
parasitic organisms, 37
parvorder, 11
peccaries, 14
Peru, 19, 29
Peruvian spider monkey, 19
pet liability policy, 40
pet trade, 13, 15, 27
Physical Characteristics, 14
Pitheciidae, 12
populations, 27, 80
prehensile tails, 12, 17, 46, 64
Primate Sanctuaries, 102
Primate Vet, 76
primates, 11, 12, 13, 14, 29, 30, 39, 52
prosimians, 11
PVC piping, 24
pygmy mouse lemur, 11
rabies, 75
rain forest, 13, 14, 15, 27, 45, 46, 63, 66, 78
Red-faced spider monkey, 19
redness, 76
Regulations, 96, 101
Reproduction, 78
rescue group, 35, 44
Rescue Groups, 29
respiratory distress, 76
sakis, 12
sanitary supplies, 36, 84
separation anxiety, 26

Index

sexual maturity, 15, 22, 26, 34, 45, 71, 78
siamangs, 11
Signs of Illness and Disease, 74
Sleeping Boxes, 66
social isolation, 26
Social Structure, 21
South, 11, 19, 20, 29, 62, 100
spayed, 81
Species Survival Plans (SSP), 29
spider monkey babies, 31, 37
Spider Monkey Habitat, 62
Spider monkeys, 14, 16
spinal cord injuries, 38
squirrel monkeys, 12
Stress, 25, 26
suspensory feeding, 14, 24, 47, 50
swelling, 76
tamarins, 12
tarsiers, 12
Television and Music, 66
terrestrial, 12, 14
tetanus, 73, 75
The Association of Zoos and Aquariums, 29
The San Diego Zoo Global program, 29
Threat Displays, 16
titis, 12
Tooth Removal, 70
Toys, 53, 65
tuberculosis, 43, 73, 75
U.K., 79, 92, 101, 102
U.K. Regulations, 101
U.S., 29, 39, 41, 42, 44, 79, 94, 96, 102, 107
U.S. Department of Agriculture's Animal and Plant Health Inspection Services, 42
uakaris, 12
United Kingdom, 10, 39, 42, 81, 96
United States, 10, 29, 39, 40, 74, 79, 80, 81, 96
Vaccinations, 75
Variegated Spider Monkey, 28
vegetables, 48, 49, 50, 51, 59
Vegetables, 48
Venezuela, 19, 20
Vertical Space, 46, 63
Vet, 76
vet clinic, 76
Veterinary Testing, 74
Vitamin D, 45
vocabulary, 37
Vocalizations, 16, 104
Water, 50, 66
white-bellied, 19
White-cheeked spider monkey, 20
White-cheeked Spider Monkey, 28
White-fronted spider monkey, 19
woolly monkeys, 12
Yucatan spider monkey, 21
zoo, 24, 26, 27, 29, 68, 69, 72
zoo exhibits, 23
Zoonotic Disease, 72
Zupreem Dry Primate Diet, 50

Published by IMB Publishing 2014

Copyright and Trademarks. This publication is Copyright 2014 by IMB Publishing. All products, publications, software and services mentioned and recommended in this publication are protected by trademarks. In such instance, all trademarks & copyright belong to the respective owners.

All rights reserved. No part of this book may be reproduced or transferred in any form or by any means, graphic, electronic, or mechanical, including photocopying, recording, taping, or by any information storage retrieval system, without the written permission of the author. Pictures used in this book are either royalty free pictures bought from stock-photo websites or have the source mentioned underneath the picture.

Disclaimer and Legal Notice. This product is not legal or medical advice and should not be interpreted in that manner. You need to do your own due-diligence to determine if the content of this product is right for you. The author and the affiliates of this product are not liable for any damages or losses associated with the content in this product. While every attempt has been made to verify the information shared in this publication, neither the author nor the affiliates assume any responsibility for errors, omissions or contrary interpretation of the subject matter herein. Any perceived slights to any specific person(s) or organization(s) are purely unintentional.

We have no control over the nature, content and availability of the web sites listed in this book. The inclusion of any web site links does not necessarily imply a recommendation or endorse the views expressed within them. IMB Publishing takes no responsibility for, and will not be liable for, the websites being temporarily unavailable or being removed from the internet. The accuracy and completeness of information provided herein and opinions stated herein are not guaranteed or warranted to produce any particular results, and the advice and strategies, contained herein may not be suitable for every individual. The author shall not be liable for any loss incurred as a consequence of the use and application, directly or indirectly, of any information presented in this work. This publication is designed to provide information in regards to the subject matter covered.

www.ingramcontent.com/pod-product-compliance
Lightning Source LLC
Chambersburg PA
CBHW060844050426
42453CB00008B/814